Lean Potion #9

COMMUNICATION:
THE NEXT LEAN FRONTIER

Sam Yankelevitch
With Claire F. Kuhl

ACKNOWLEDGEMENTS

The Long List

I would like to thank everyone I have encountered in life. This of course includes family, friends, business coworkers, and gurus. You know who you are and the significant influence each of you has had on my growth. Please keep up your kind support.

Big hugs and kisses to my wife for her love and understanding while I wrote this book.

The Short List

Thanks to:

Claire F. Kuhl, my ghostwriter and editor, who was instrumental in being able to grasp my wandering thoughts and nail them down into a concise and entertaining story form. I am thankful for her skill, discipline, and oodles of patience. Her understanding of lean concepts and communication were absolute keys to being able to accomplish this work. The illustrations, which abide by the Keep it Simple rule, are also Claire's.

Chris Klasing, who has been my friend and lean mentor for many years. Chris reviewed a manuscript I wrote several years ago and thanks to his candor, I decided to keep my day job for several more years. His insights and review on the ideas we present were of huge value.

Craig Long, Jerry Bussell, and Eric Hayler, who provided excellent comments, critique and feedback. I realize how busy you are and truly appreciate the candor and encouragement provided by such well-versed lean practitioners as yourselves.

The team at Wavecloud and my project contact Sarah Busby, who has a good deal of tolerance, patience, and the required good humor to make it happen. She supported the work albeit our constant surprises and changes.

Vito Giordano and his masterful ways of coaching which inspired me to attempt the subject of communication seriously. Jane Allen, CEO of Smart Work Network-for introducing Vito and Claire to me and providing years of friendship and support.

Deb Sofield, my expert speech coach and author of Speak Without Fear and Gil Gerretsen, President of BizTrek who drove me through his no-nonsense Fastlane Marketing program.

TABLE OF CONTENTS

PREFACE

The Communication Challenge

For more than thirty years, the tenets of
The Toyota Way and lean manufacturing have
been transforming the way that companies think
about how they design processes, build products,
and manage supply chains. Today, the time has
come for lean practitioners and promoters—*like
you!*—to tackle the *next* frontier of waste, rework,
and frustration: **communication**.

In our increasingly complex world, a
huge percentage of companies and supply
chains require people to surmount multiple
barriers that deter them from achieving true
understanding and agreement. The occasional
lapse in communication may *seem* trivial, but the
ramifications can be stunning. Consider the case
of the Airbus A380.

Case 1: Airbus's Billion-Dollar Bungle

The Airbus A380 is the world's largest commercial aircraft. Although it is now quite popular, the A380 got off to a rocky start. It was scheduled for delivery in 2006; however, the aircraft's entry into service was delayed almost two years and the project was estimated to be as much as *6.1 billion* **dollars over budget.**

What happened? It was a classic **failure to communicate** effectively, and a triumph of wishful thinking over reality. The development of the aircraft was a collaboration among sixteen sites spread across four different countries—except they didn't *really* manage to collaborate very well. For example, German and Spanish designers used CATIA Version 4 design software, while British and French teams had upgraded to Version 5.

As it turns out, CATIA V5 wasn't just a small upgrade from CATIA V4—it was a *total rewrite* that changed some of the key algorithms used, including the one that provided values to compensate wiring harness lengths for the bend radii. This is an absolutely crucial calculation, because wiring systems that have to be installed inside an airplane fuselage must account for all the bends and turns that make up the geometry inside the airframe. Wires and harness bundles wind around obstacles or sit on top of each other, creating minor differences in length because of all those curves.

When it came time to build the prototype, the various design groups contributed their wiring diagrams and specifications, and suppliers built the wiring harnesses according to the specifications they received. But when the harnesses were installed, to everyone's horror, many of the bundles were too short. The reason? The two versions of CATIA calculated those bend radii differently, making the specifications unreliable. Even a few millimeters' difference here and there becomes disastrous when you are dealing with 530 kilometers (330 miles) of wiring.

Thousands of man-hours were lost to redesign and rework, accounting for major monetary losses, numerous order cancellations, and severe damage to Airbus's reputation.

So how does something like this happen? Why did someone decide to plunge ahead with the project, knowing that the computer systems couldn't talk to each other? For that matter, it was difficult for the *people* to talk to each other. English was chosen as the official language of the project, even though the majority of participants were *not* native English speakers.

> When different parts of an organization can't communicate effectively with each other to resolve differences and make reasonable decisions, waste is present, and *everybody* loses.

The root cause is that Airbus was torn by internal wrangling dating back to a series of past mergers. Different parts of the organization inherited different corporate cultures, management styles, and IT systems. Even at the very top of the organization, there was an elaborate split between French and German control. Personal rivalries and national pride are reported to have been issues that stood in the way, and pressure to keep the project moving forward meant that the CATIA software version disparity was never resolved.

When different parts of an organization can't communicate effectively with each other to resolve differences and make reasonable decisions, waste is present and *everybody* **loses**. For Airbus, it was $6.1 billion of waste.

Obviously, not every communication problem creates losses of this magnitude, but as lean protocols teach us, *any* non-value-add situation is ripe for removal or reduction. Consider this example from my own manufacturing experience.

Case 2: Raphael's Take-Down Mix-Up

One Friday, my leadership team and I were meeting to plan a preventive maintenance

overhaul on one of our plant's aluminum
extrusion presses, scheduled to take place that
weekend. I called in Raphael[1], our junior plant
maintenance man.

"Hey, Raphael, the guys are going to be working
on the extrusion press tomorrow. Would you be
sure to take down the breakers, so we don't have
any accidents?"

"Sure, boss. No problem!"

Now, for all of us sitting in the meeting, this
was a perfectly clear request for a simple, yet
crucial, safety step that needed to be taken.
But when I came in the next day, I saw a large
metal panel sitting in a corner of our operations
meeting room.

Raphael did exactly what we asked: he took
down the breakers. Instead of simply flipping
the breakers down to the Off position, Raphael
unbolted the whole panel to truly take them
down off the wall.

---

[1] Names have been changed to protect the confused.

That's a communication breakdown, all right! And it represents just one of the many ways that communication efforts can go off the rails.

By applying the transformative power of lean thinking[2] in your organization's communication process, you can help all players spot a breakdown situation and solve it. Lean tools exist to improve processes, any processes, including those associated with communication.

Just imagine the benefits of working in a company that *consistently* operates in a mode of lean communication; i.e., communication that correctly conveys meaning, attains shared understanding, achieves clear actions, and produces results that are aligned with expectations, goals, and objectives. And where everyone involved has a mechanism and tools that protect them from falling back into the *old* habits, which have a lot of inherent error and waste.

This is where communication *adds* value.

---

[2] *Lean Thinking* is the title of Womack and Jones' seminal book; see the Bibliography.

Now take this idea a step further, and try picturing what your personal life would be like if there were no more miscommunications, misunderstandings, and mishaps to create turmoil in your relationships.

Most companies—and certainly most families—do not have agreed-upon approaches to analyzing and discussing how to identify all the waste, costs, and other negative consequences associated with communication problems. Wouldn't it be *magical* if such an approach existed?

I submit to you that lean thinking has the potential to *be* that approach. The lean philosophy brings with it a suite of familiar tools and methodologies that you mastered for use in a manufacturing context. But twist your paradigm just slightly, and you can apply those same constructs to communication. Like magic, you've got a whole new set of tools for ensuring that message and meaning are conveyed without confusion, that understanding is truly shared by all concerned, and that the actions you plan are executed exactly as you envisioned them to accomplish their intended purpose.

Who Should Read This Book?

Lean Potion #9 is written *primarily* to persuade people who are already involved in lean manufacturing to expand their thinking and apply lean techniques more broadly. By *involved*, I mean lean practitioners, of course, but also the CEOs, middle managers, and other lean champions throughout the organization who appreciate the benefits that lean has brought to your processes and your pocketbook. My challenge to you all is to embrace lean thinking as a way to improve communication, both at work and in life.

As a lean practitioners and advocates, you have a huge advantage over many other players in your organization: you are adept at using proven tools, a specific language, and well-documented standards to determine what is or is *not* adding value in a given process or situation. (Indeed,

because of your background, the majority of this
book assumes that you have a general knowledge
of lean philosophies, tools and language.)

> Lean culture uses proven tools, a specific
> language, and well-documented standards to
> determine what is or is *not* adding value in a
> given process or situation.

Lean practitioners are trained in identifying
and allowing waste to come to the surface. By
uncovering areas of potential waste, we are able to
see, describe, and solve. As you well know, "Out
of sight, out of mind." By design, lean allows, even
expects, ugly things to surface, so they can be dealt
with effectively and permanently. Lean actually
accelerates change and drives companies toward
performance excellence.

Of course, lean practitioners cannot conquer
communication challenges *alone!*

So if you're just curious about lean, or if you've
been recruited by a proactive lean thinker to
join his or her quest to lead change, you'll find

Lean Lingo sidebars along the way to clarify
some of the key concepts that are fundamental
to understanding how lean works. If you *really*
get hooked on lean, like I did, you may want
to plunge into some of the books listed in the
Bibliography. And you can always rely on lean
practitioners around you to serve as mentors,
guides, and translators as you explore the
lean landscape.

Who Am I to Write This Book?

When you name the Really Big Names in the
lean pantheon, *Sam Yankelevitch* doesn't come up.
So who am I, and where did I get the nerve to
write a book about lean?

I'm just one of thousands of professionals
who have been living and promoting the lean
manufacturing mindset since the mid-1980s.
As you'll see, learning about lean completely
transformed my approach to business, and I
immediately became a relentless advocate for
applying lean philosophies in my own company.

Now, after almost three decades of seeing first-hand what lean thinking can do, I decided to continue looking for creative ways to apply lean thinking beyond the boundaries of the shop floor.

But I'm getting ahead of myself. Let me tell you about how I first stumbled into lean thinking, and how it became the basis for my approach to business and life at almost every level.

Years ago, as happens with most young people, the time came for me to make a decision about going to college. Where would I go? What major would be right for me? And how would I know?

Also like most young people, I thought about potential jobs and career-path opportunities. In my specific case, my grandfather was the founder and owner of a very successful lock and hardware manufacturing company in Colombia, South America. He and the family hoped that I would decide to work there and eventually run it.

Well, that sounded good to me! So I chose Industrial Engineering for my major, and studied at the University of Texas at Arlington, graduating in 1981. The curriculum at that time included a lot of time and motion studies, and batch production methodologies. Lots of Fredrick Taylor's theories.

University life focused on the theoretical. I spent my time manipulating little paper cut-outs to mock-up plant layouts and using punch cards in the computer room to generate process simulations. Upon graduation, it was quite a jolt to jump straight into a bustling real, live tool shop in Grandpa's plant.

The shop floor back then was set up in a typical department-by-department structure and everything was processed in batches. Services were centralized, including the tool shop where I was frantically trying to master the realities of our business. I saw masses of people and material moving from one end of the line to the other—long cycle times, lots and *lots* of inventory, plenty of bottlenecks, and a flow that was punctuated with constant stops and starts.

But that was the way the business had been run since the early 1950s, and it was reasonably profitable. So that's what I learned and understood to be the way things *should* be. I really felt no need to question things…until one fateful day in 1985.

Our company had just started expanding our export business to include Mexico. One of the new Mexican customers flew in to visit our factory. At some point during the tour, and for reasons I may never understand, this gentleman reached into his attaché case, took out a book, and handed it to me, saying, "Sam, somebody gave me this darn book the other day, and I *really* don't understand what it's about. I'm thinking maybe a young up-and-comer like you can figure it out." The book was *The Goal*, by Eliyahu Goldratt.

WOW! Goldratt's approach *completely* blew my mind!

Suddenly, some of the situations we'd been struggling with popped into a new focus. I began questioning the fundamentals I'd assumed were carved in stone, and, being hungry to learn more, searched for more literature related to the topic. (Mind you, this was in the days *before* Google or Amazon—I actually had to visit libraries and bookstores!) Once I started digging, I unearthed a few more revolutionary books, a handful of titles that all related to the Toyota Production System.

Fortunately for me, the books were loaded with examples and illustrations that brought to life the disarmingly simple, yet powerful, philosophies that Toyota was implementing. As I had already surmised, many of the theories I had studied so hard in college would have to go out the window to let in the fresh air of what I was learning—things like continuous flow, cellular design, and waste reduction methodologies—that would much later be referred to as *lean thinking*.

Being a brash young fellow, I pulled the manufacturing engineer, some supervisors, and

a few operators into my confidence, sold them
on the new lean approach, and set out to test the
theories in one specific product group: die-cast
plumbing products. (In retrospect, they *may* have
gone along with my schemes more because I was
the owner's grandson, and less because of my
eloquence as a lean spokesperson.)

The die-cast plumbing line was a target-rich
environment: high inventories, 45-day cycle
times, quality problems, and way too much scrap.
Applying what we'd learned from our reading, we
redesigned the layout to create a continuous flow
cell. Once the new cell ramped up, we immediately
saw the constraints and how they contributed, one
way or another, to the dismal performance and
quality problems we'd been experiencing.

With the basics in place, we experimented,
tweaked, measured, tweaked some more, and
ultimately exceeded even *my* expectations for
what the new approach could achieve. Through
the transformative power of lean, even at this
rudimentary level, we eliminated weeks of cycle

time while minimizing scrap and maximizing quality. You could say that in our new die-cast plumbing cell, the "water" was no longer leaking out through the seals, but flowing though the spout, as intended.

Throughout my career at the Colombia plant, we persevered in changing and improving our manufacturing processes through the adoption of lean-based philosophies. I must admit that, even though we did not implement a complete lean system or fully sustain the efforts we initiated, the benefits were evident, and the profitability of the company improved dramatically.

Since those early wins, my interest in lean has grown until it permeates my approach to every process, inside and outside of the manufacturing department. In every job and assignment, I have, in some way or another, driven or participated in lean activities and implementation.

Over my years of participating in and promoting this incredible system and philosophy, I've seen over and over that selling lean concepts and implementing them across multicultural environments are challenges in themselves. Anyone anywhere who believes that there's a cookie-cutter, cut 'n' paste way to shortcut lean implementation is going to receive a rude awakening.

The concepts of lean are simple, but implementation requires hard work. Once you've had that "Aha!" moment, you'll need persistent discipline and mental rigor to attain success. The lean concepts have to be carefully and thoughtfully assimilated if they are going to be transplanted successfully from one cultural environment to another. Attempts to short-circuit this hard work will result in a journey that is longer, more painful, and more *muda*-ful than it needs to be. What works in one corporate culture or one part of the world may not work in another.

Lean Lingo

Muda= Japanese/lean term for *waste*.

The lean journey is always long and intense, and sustainable success comes only when the actual people who do the actual work grasp each situation and willingly implement a better way of doing things.

So who am I to write this book? A veteran and a true believer who is confident that now is the time to focus the magic of lean on conquering the next frontier—how to use this incredible continuous improvement system to deal with the realities of **communicating effectively** in today's business world, with its long and complex supply chains.

I offer to you the three key insights that have emerged during my contemplation of applying lean thinking to improving communication:

- The more **complex** a work environment becomes, the more important it is for all parties to communicate effectively.
- Communication is a **process**.
- The transformative power of lean thinking and **continuous improvement** can be

applied to any process; therefore, it's time for lean practitioners and champions to take on the challenge of making communication in your company more effective.

Consider this your official call to action!

Why *Lean* Potion #9?

By the way, you may be wondering where I got the title for this book—especially if you're under the age of fifty. When I was a kid, a song called "Love Potion #9"[3] was extremely popular. In the song, the singer drinks a gypsy's potion and suddenly sees the whole world differently, to the point where he kisses the policeman on the corner.

To me, learning to "think lean" has much the same effect—things that looked normal before suddenly look different now. Lean makes it possible for us to see things that we previously could not see, for the invisible to become visible. We lose our fear of the unknown as our lean superpowers kick

---

[3] "Love Potion #9." Lyrics by Jerry Lieber and Mike Stoller. 1959. © Sony/ATV Tunes, LLC.

in, unleashing innate curiosity and compelling
us to think differently about what was formerly
assumed to be the inevitable norm.

When I speak of lean thinking as a "magic
potion," I'm also thinking of the enormous power
you can leverage when you embrace the point of
view that there is *always* a better way to do things.

So, fellow practitioners and proponents, let's take
the familiar ingredients of lean manufacturing
and brew up a *new* potion that will help us see our
communication practices differently and begin the
process of continuously improving them ***now***.

CHAPTER 1
COST OF COMPLEXITY

You've heard it—or said it—a million times:
"Keep it simple, stupid." Great advice, but not
always doable in today's 24/7/365 global economy.
Political changes have opened the door to long-
distance trade relationships that were unthinkable
in the past. Even had they been thinkable, it's
only in the past twenty years or so that advances
in technology have made it practical for average
companies to build just-in-time supply chains and
distribution channels that span the globe.

> The more *complex* a work environment
> becomes, the more important it is for all
> parties to communicate effectively.

Of course, as soon as you have multinational
business networks, you have the additional
complications of cultural and linguistic

differences. And all that added geographical distance makes lead times longer. Even today, it takes more than thirty days for a ship to cross the Pacific Ocean, versus waiting an hour for a truck to carry components thirty miles from across town.

> The *world* is the new shop floor.

Shorter lead times allow for faster solutions. Cause and effect are closer together.

The more **complex** a work environment becomes, the more important it is for all parties to communicate effectively. Orville and Wilbur probably didn't have too much trouble reconciling their engineering drawings for the first airplane or agreeing on adjustments to a particular component after testing it.

The Airbus people found things to be a *bit* more challenging. First, they were dealing with an engineering marvel of staggering complexity. The electrical system alone comprised more than 100,000 wires and 40,300 connectors performing 1,150 separate functions. The team struggled to share ideas, refine designs, and make decisions while working across sixteen sites located in four different countries with four different native languages and customs, reflecting two not-well-merged corporate cultures. And, of course, there was the issue of the incompatible software releases.

According to Andrea Rothman, writing for Bloomberg.com in 2006:

"...engineers in Germany and Spain stuck with an earlier version of Paris-based Dassault Systemes SA's CATIA design software, even though the French and British offices had upgraded to CATIA 5. That meant the German teams couldn't add their design changes for the electrical wiring back into the common three-dimensional digital mockup being produced in Toulouse, Champion says. Efforts to fiddle with the software to make it compatible failed, meaning that changes to the designs in the two offices couldn't be managed and integrated in real time, he says. The situation worsened when construction and tests of the first A380s generated demands for structural changes that would affect the wiring. The changes in configuration had to be made manually **because the software tools couldn't *talk* to each other[4].**"

Manually changing the configuration for 100,000 wires and 40,300 connectors?!? You don't need a degree in probability to predict problems when dealing with that many potential points of failure.

In my experience, you don't even have to be at that extreme level of complexity to encounter costly problems. Let's consider how "complexity creep" affects communication efforts.

The Early Days at Toyota

In the earliest days, when lean concepts were first emerging at Toyota, the supply chain was very local—Japanese client and Japanese suppliers sharing one language, one set of cultural norms. Most of the suppliers were within a fifty-mile

[4] Emphasis added.

radius of the assembly plant. That helped keep lead times short, which made the concept of pull strategy and just-in-time inventory quite workable.

Lean Lingo

The Seven Forms of *Muda*:
- Over-production
- Inventory
- Motion
- Waiting
- Conveyance
- Over-processing
- Non-right first time

Any communication issues they had were probably minimal compared to all the other sources of *muda* that they were discovering and battling. This *muda* later became categorized in the now well-known seven types of waste for manufacturing environments. And you'll note that they found all of this even in their compact universe of short distances, short lead-times, shared language, and common culture.

New World, New Lean

Fast forward sixty years. Consider now the challenges and opportunities of globalization, and the impact it has on companies and people. The world is the new shop floor!

Although it's been around for a while, globalization has accelerated significantly over the past several years, compounding the collision of cultures and customs, and creating whole *new* communication hurdles.

As companies and supply chains grow ever larger and more complex, they present their people with barrier after barrier that block true understanding and agreement. A great number of twenty-first century products depend on materials and components fabricated thousands of miles away from where they are assembled. To navigate each component through its many stops on the road to the final customer takes constant interaction between people and systems.

Possibilities for miscommunication among people abound. Certainly, people from different cultures and backgrounds who speak different languages may encounter challenges in coordinating

multiple products across continents and time
zones. But even beyond international and ethnic
barriers, remember that all too often, the Baby
Boomers don't understand the Millennials. The
men don't understand the women. The bosses
don't understand the workers. The driven Type A's
don't understand the laid-back Type B's. And the
list goes on.

> Communication is the next frontier for lean
> implementation in our global supply chain.

As the Airbus story has already highlighted,
systems and technologies also encounter
difficulties in trying to share information. Do we
need EDI or XML to share ERP data? Can your
PC handle my Mac files? Can we both maintain
your cloud-based database in real time? Can you
run this Apple app on your Android? Again, the
list goes on.

Despite the difficulties, effective communication
is absolutely essential. So how do we overcome
these gaps?

> The same continuous improvement
> methodologies we have learned and adopted
> from Toyota can also detect communication
> *muda* that has crept in because of globalization
> and increasing complexity.

Fortunately, the same continuous improvement methodologies we have learned and adopted from Toyota can also detect communication *muda* that has crept in because of globalization and increasing complexity. If we focus our "new" lean thinking on communication at the operational level, where things actually get done, we should be able to have a significant positive impact on actions and performance.

Lean, when it becomes the cultural communication norm, can be a bridge to overcome barriers and build connections among different stakeholders, regardless of their origins, background, and upbringing. In this book, we'll explore how to embed lean communications into an organization.

For now, envision the end result of working in a culture with where lean communication practices are fully in play:

- Every conversation[5] ultimately has the customer in mind and contains as little waste as possible—focus on adding value for the customer

- Listening and reflecting back for confirmation and clarity are considered to be essential elements of every conversation—"Seek first to understand, and then to be understood"

- Every stakeholder takes responsibility for learning from results that are less than perfect to make them better the next time (and nothing is *ever* perfect)—continuous process improvement

- Each individual is valued by the group, and the group is valued by each individual—"All for one and one for all!"

---

[5] Note that throughout this book, the word *conversation* refers to any exchange of information, person-to-person or system-to-system, whether via spoken or written word, diagram, data feed, etc.

Communication is the next frontier for lean implementation in our global supply chain. Lean wisdom teaches us that you are only as effective as the weakest supplier in the chain. In the same way, your collaboration and execution are only as effective as the weakest communicator in the conversation.

"But wait!" you may say. "How can tools and rules intended for a manufacturing assembly line possibly pertain to something as intangible as communication?"

Fundamentally, lean tools are designed to improve processes. A manufacturing assembly line is, very obviously, a process. Step One of the process adds value and yields a result that becomes the input to Step Two of the process. Step Two takes that input, adds value, and produces a result that is the input to Step Three. And so on and so on until the final result/deliverable/product is ready.

So how about communication? Does it proceed in definable steps that yield results? Can those steps and results be improved? Is communication a process? If it is, then forward-thinking practitioners like you should be able to wield the transformative power of lean to continuously improve communication efforts and make them yield better results. The next section addresses this crucial question.

CHAPTER 2
COMMUNICATION *IS* A PROCESS

In his profoundly influential book, *The 7 Habits of Highly Effective People®*, Stephen R. Covey states, "…all things are created twice. There's a mental or first creation, and a physical or second creation to all things."

First Creation   Second Creation

Every day, you think of hundreds of things and execute them without any help at all. You sail along, the star of your own movie, and that's great.

But you also have ideas that you cannot execute alone. Lots of ideas, in fact, especially in the world of business. It turns out that John Donne was right when he said, "No man is an island." As soon as you have to engage even one more person in transforming your idea into reality, you've got to deal with some form of **communication.** And as we know all too well, this is not always straightforward or easy.

Building on Covey's concept of multiple creations, the act of communication actually requires a *third* creation, the sender's meaning created in the mind of the receiver, and a *fourth* creation, the receiver executing in the physical realm.

> For an idea to become reality, it first begins with a thought in someone's mind. The thought needs to be *conveyed* in order for action to occur.

As a manufacturing maven, I instantly see this series of transactions as a *process.*

Aha!

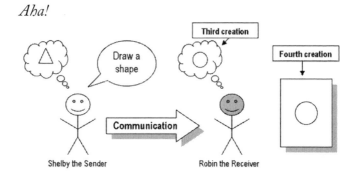

Shelby the Sender   Robin the Receiver

Communication *is* a process. Ergo, lean thinking can be applied to make our communication efforts more productive, less error-prone, and even more enjoyable.

Even with just two people interacting, you can bet that the communication process is going to hit some snags along the way, and the original idea may not be executed as originally conceived. The more people you add, the messier things get.

Variance = Process Improvement Opportunity

Basic communication theory attempts to explain how a message is sent out (in this case, by Shelby the Sender), and how it is received by another person (Robin the Receiver). In all too many cases, for a variety of reasons, the original idea transmitted by the sender is not correctly understood by the receiver. The difference between the originally intended idea and the interpreted idea is a difference in meaning.

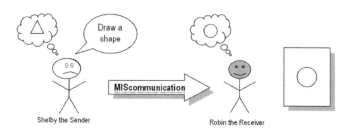

 is not equal

In our diagram, the meaning that Robin received (shape = circle) is not the meaning that Shelby had in mind (shape = triangle). When Robin draws the shape, the outcome of this particular communication process is not what Shelby originally

---

Lean Lingo

One definition of *quality* is conformance to a standard. When an item does not match the standard, a *variance* exists.

---

intended. In other words, the executed idea doesn't match the standard of the original idea. A variance exists.

Meaning A ≠ Meaning B = Variance = Opportunity for improvement

The communication process adds value *only* if the meaning being conveyed is shared by the sender and all receivers. When meanings differ, we have *non*-value-added effort.

In a work environment—whether manufacturing, service, or other industry—things get done by people who are communicating constantly, conveying messages to each other, receiving feedback from each other and from their observations of the results of their communication efforts.

If the messages being exchanged are intended to drive performance and execution—get things done—there would be significant benefit in somehow ensuring that the meanings being continuously exchanged are always understood as clearly as possible. Ideally, there would be no variance between the sent message and the received message.

More than Words Can Say

In our little example, Shelby the Sender and Robin the Receiver communicated via spoken word. But obviously, communication processes in the real world involve many channels—memos, drawings, videos, documents, body language, vocal inflection, and of course, emails, emails, and more emails. The communication process may take place entirely in real time between parties in the same location, or may require conveying ideas across long time periods and great distances. Communication processes don't necessarily even involve human-to-human contact. Sometimes our technologies and systems manage to mangle messages for us as data moves across applications and platforms. The channel doesn't matter—communication is still a process that can (and usually should) be improved.

For example, in our complex business worlds, we often communicate via documents, diagrams, and IT systems. Engineering drawings and operating instructions are common ways to convey a message. The challenge: can this be done clearly enough to ensure that the meaning of the information conveyed on such documents is received accurately by every intended recipient?

All too often, the mission is *not* accomplished, resulting in multiple rounds of clarification and conveyance between departments and companies.

For example, a Tier 2 automotive supplier where I worked frequently received product specifications via a print or an engineering drawing. On many occasions, the prints we received were either missing critical details or included misleading information.

Knowing this could happen, we stayed on the alert, and relied on an internal team of engineers to review prints as they arrived. When they found something questionable, they transmitted the details of the question or correction to the customer for their review and response.

The customer, often after weeks of reworking the prints, would send a new set of drawings to us, which would kick off yet another review by our team to ensure that all the details needed for proper execution were included. Clearly, this was a process that needed some serious improvement.

To add even more complexity to situations like this, technical drawings and engineering prints many times refer to specifications, norms, and other standards that may be company-, industry-, or even country-specific with details available only in the language of that country.

In today's globalized supply chain, such drawings are translated and used across the world. Because translations are mostly interpretations, time and money are lost in attempts to guess the intent and expectation that is being conveyed. In such cases, it is not uncommon for cautious companies to print a caveat on the drawing: "When in doubt, consult the original German [*or Japanese or whatever*] version of the document." This in itself acknowledges the probability of things being lost in translation and creating miscommunication errors.

In another real-life experience, a local company transferred an automation line from its US plant to one of the facilities in Mexico. The work instructions were compiled and written by the US engineering team and sent out for translation to Spanish. Once the line arrived in Mexico, it took several weeks longer than expected to assemble the line and ramp it up. The delays resulted in lost productivity, late deliveries, and a furious customer.

So what caused these costly delays?

As it turned out, the translated version was very difficult for the Mexican crew to follow. Not every translator can handle the unique language requirements of a specialized discipline. Also, details taken for granted on the US side were not explicitly provided in the operating instructions. What is "common knowledge" in one setting isn't necessarily common at all in another, and we assume that it is at our own risk.

Again, regardless of the channels your communication processes use to convey messages, when those messages are intended to drive performance and execution, you and

your organization would gain significant
benefit by ensuring that the meanings are
being continuously exchanged with no variance
between the sent message and the received
message. Only then is the true value of the
communication effort realized.

What's the Value Proposition?

Wherever the communication process breaks
down, and miscommunication occurs, it almost
always leads to **non-value added** activity. And
non-value-added activity is **waste**—*muda*[6] to us
lean wizards. (That means "big bucks," whatever
language you speak)

If a single one-on-one conversation can create a little
muda, consider that most organizations comprise
multiple functional areas staffed by lots of people:
sales, customer service, finance, project management,
engineering, logistics, production control,

---

[6] For any non-lean-wizards who are reading this: Toyota Motor Corporation's
innovative Toyota Production System is credited with being the foundation for
lean manufacturing principles now applied around the world. Because Toyota
is based in Japan, the language of lean incorporates many Japanese words and
concepts.

manufacturing,
warehousing,
shipping, and so on.
Each of those
functional areas
probably has its own
layers of
management. And
at the top of the
heap are the various
Chiefs of this and
that. Just imagine all

> **Lean Lingo**
>
> "The first question...is always 'What does the customer want from this process?' (Both the internal customer at the next steps in the production line and the final, external customer.) *This defines value.*"
>
> *From The* Toyota Way, *by Jeffery K. Liker*

the attempted conversations among all those people, up, down, and across organizational lines and levels.

A process *that* complex is the perfect breeding ground for *muda!*

Even companies with wonderfully robust communication processes will still find that even one small communication glitch can drive an organization toward corrective actions that can cost big money. For efficient, effective, value-added execution to occur, conversations among all areas and individuals need to consistently convey meanings clearly, adding value to every step of every business process.

Indeed, in an ideal company, everyone involved would enjoy a continuous exchange and flow of correctly shared ideas, leading inexorably toward desired actions being performed correctly to meet customers' needs and expectations. At each communication point, the received message would match as closely as possible the meaning that the sender intended. Sender and receiver would be in *agreement*, sharing an understanding of the *standard* by which results will be evaluated.

Sadly, this *continuous flow*—another key lean concept—can be diverted, diluted, or even stopped when meanings are not shared fully and correctly, causing the business processes to yield different results than were originally intended.

Lean Lingo

Continuous flow means moving something completely through the value stream without stopping

This variance in results, this failure to achieve *standard work*, ultimately hurts the customer, both internal and external. In many ways, your top communication priority is to clearly understand your customers' expectations and requirements; otherwise, your outcomes will create waste or non-value-added results. And you won't be in business for long.

As a master of lean practices, you can save the day by mapping the stream where **communication** value is being created or not, just as surely as you've already done on the manufacturing line and in the supply chain. Douse the communication channels with a bucket of Lean Potion #9 to provide a clear picture of the situation and determine what corrections might be needed to drive the waste out of your communication processes.

At the end of the day, in any business, people and their interactions with each other—communication—lead a company to enjoy the thrill of victory or suffer the agony of defeat. The next section is offered as an initial do-it-yourself guide to applying your lean expertise in this new context.

Chapter 3
Continuously Improving
Communication Processes

As you've seen thus far, organizations working
in complex situations must overcome many
communication-related hurdles, each of which
adds cost. Happily, communication is a process,
which means that lean thinking can be applied
to make your communication efforts more
productive, less error-prone, and even more
enjoyable.

My goal in this section is to draw parallels
between the shop floor and the communications
arena while suggesting how familiar lean tools
might be applied effectively. My hope is that this
first round of ideas will stimulate *your* thinking
and serve as a springboard to you and your
company—one that moves you toward creating a

systemic set of solutions to deal with snags that exist in your communication processes. Whether you're a CEO, a manufacturing manager, or a front-line contributor, *you* can take the first step in leading the charge on lean communication.

What a Waste: Non-Value-Add

As we've already seen, communication processes are susceptible to the classic lean problems of variance and non-value-added activity. Indeed, communication processes can suffer from outbreaks of all three categories of waste:

- *Muda*—non-value-add
- *Mura*—inconsistency; uneven flow
- *Muri*—overburdening; no value added beyond capability

These three familiar lean terms can help you see and understand the different types and sources of waste in communication processes. Like the Three Musketeers of literary fame, these concepts are much more powerful when deployed as part of a unified whole. However, to better understand how each of these manifests in the communication context, it may be helpful to examine them one at a time for now.

Muda

In traditional lean thinking, the concept of waste is associated with anything that is *adding no value*—that is, does not contribute to meeting or exceeding the customer's expectations. As a lean professional, you can, I'm sure, recite the seven (plus one) wastes without batting an eye:

- Over-Production
- Inventory
- Wasted Motion
- Waiting
- Conveyance
- Over-Processing
- Non-Right First Time (i.e., scrap, rework, and defects)
- Under-Utilization of People

You can also undoubtedly cite plenty of examples of how you have reduced or eliminated these dreaded elements from your manufacturing processes. But what do these familiar villains look like in a communication context? Let's consider a few tales of communication *muda*.

Over-Production

In the communication context, over-production occurs in any conversation that delivers too much information, delivers it before it could possibly be useful, and/or redirects focus away from what the "customer" actually wanted. One example can be found in the classic description of that frustrating co-worker who talks all around the point without ever getting to it: "Whenever I ask that guy what time it is, he tells me how to build a clock!"

Inventory

A management consultant I know was asked to help a client organize her company's online documentation library. For years, employees had created folders and saved files willy-nilly, using neither naming standards nor agreed-upon organizing principles.

In one extreme case, the consultant found a dozen slightly different versions of the same procedure document. And because no one bothered to even put dates on the documents (never mind enforcing document control!), it was impossible to determine which version was the most current. Clearly, the time and money invested in creating this inventory of stale and unreliable documents was wasted.

Wasted Motion

On the production line, wasted motion occurs when individuals perform more steps than necessary to complete a process. Here's a classic example of extra steps in a communication context.

It's typical these days to have different IT systems "talk" to each other to exchange and compare data. Obviously, the intent of having such set-ups would be to leave the number-crunching to machines rather than humans. After all, machines are cheaper and, if properly programmed, make fewer errors.

I recently heard the story of an automobile OEM that used their student interns as a "low cost" alternative to reviewing and correcting the output of two different IT systems. The systems were supposed to communicate with each other to control the specific components that were going to be assembled on a car, based on the features ordered. Apparently, the systems were *not* properly programmed and did *not* communicate according to specifications. Therefore, the students were directed to download the output from the two systems into spreadsheets, manipulate the data, and then reenter it into a *third* local system to drive the final assembly of a vehicle.

What a nightmare of wasted motion! The process now loops through multiple extra steps, people, and systems. Data is moving onto and off of platforms unnecessarily. And the whole approach almost seems designed to maximize the introduction of errors, omissions, and variance of all types into the process. When the decision was made to use the "low cost" intern solution, did anyone calculate the *actual* ROI after wasted motion and variances were addressed?

Waiting

Back in the 1980s, a large information processing company in Chicago got the Total Quality Management bug. Before long, everyone there was going to training classes on process improvement theory and techniques. Fishbone diagrams started appearing on the walls, and even front-line folks were asking The Five Whys and pursuing The Three Actuals.

The CEO was a real champion for the changes, and urged his executive team to analyze *their* processes and look for improvement opportunities. They decided to tackle the question of why they spent so much time in meetings.

Much to the CEO's chagrin, root-cause analysis revealed that *waiting for him to arrive* was the #1 reason for late starts and lost productivity in his team's meetings. He was suitably appalled when the team tallied up the cost of their collective salaries for the hours lost to the waiting game.

Wrangling procedural red tape can also create costly wait-times. Our automotive supply chain was struggling with on-time delivery and with quality issues in working with a particular customer. The relationship was structured such that

---

Lean Lingo

Fishbone diagram— graphical tool for analyzing cause and effect in a process; also known as an Ishikawa diagram

The Five Whys— technique for finding the root cause of a problem by repeatedly asking "Why?"

The Three Actuals— technique for analyzing a process by going to the actual place and observing the actual people doing the actual work

the customer had to provide an approved Purchase Order to kick off the next step of each project.

In our root-cause analysis, we interviewed several project managers and quality personnel and determined that the problems resulted from *waiting* for the PO to arrive. The customer would often send it too late in the timeline, creating lots of last-minute rushing through critical details. Not surprisingly, this resulted in quality lapses, missed deadlines, and ultimately, large amounts of money wasted.

Goldratt's Theory of Constraints[7] teaches us that the problems of waiting create costs that will never be recovered when these are directly associated with a bottleneck. When deadlines aren't met early in a process, the waiting game downstream causes non-value-add activities and their associated costs.

Conveyance and Handling

On the assembly line, no value is added when a part has to be moved from one end of a building to the other end. It is implicit also that in processes

---

[7] See "Finding the Bottleneck: The Theory of Constraints" on page 158.

that move parts unnecessarily, those parts are handled over and over, and each touch-point is an opportunity for a quality problem. Similar issues can occur when conveying messages.

A large Tier 1 supplier received notification from the OEM that engineering changes were needed to some design drawings. The notification included the critical, specific detail of **when** the new revision would be implemented. The message was conveyed to the Tier 2 supplier, who in turn conveyed the message to the sub-suppliers.

In response, groups of people started talking with other groups of people, and numerous project meetings and cross-functional global team meetings were convened to convey the status of the engineering change. The crucial detail of the launch date was conveyed with relatively little importance, compared to the technical details for the engineering change needed.

In this particular case, the hefty amount of information-handling across tiers and teams opened an opportunity for a junior engineer at one sub-supplier to change a crucial piece of data: the authorized launch date. He misread the date because of the difference between American-style dates (*mm/dd/yy*) versus European- and Latin American-style dates (*dd/mm/yy*).[8] As a result, tooling and materials were switched over to the new version prematurely.

Next scene: when the Tier 1 started receiving the new version at their dock, contrary to the original instructions, *quite* a few pointed (to the point of being unprintable, perhaps) messages were conveyed in late-night phone calls with top management from the entire supply chain.

Over-Processing

Here's a great illustration of over-processing that I heard from a consultant and friend with whom I enjoy swapping war stories:

---

[8] The expected due-date of October 8, 2012 was misunderstood to be August 10, 2012.

When I worked at an information processing firm
in Chicago, I had a terrific individual reporting to
me by the name of Pat. Pat was as sharp as they
come, highly responsive, and extremely diligent in
her approach to work.

In a departmental meeting, my boss, the CIO,
asked Pat if she knew how much it would cost to
move one of our documentation processes off of
paper and onto an online platform. When she said
no, he shrugged and moved on.

Later in the week, Pat came in for her regular
status meeting with me.

"So how are things going, Pat?"

"Well, I'm a little behind on some of my work
because I wanted to focus on the big new project
from the CIO."

"*What* big new project?! Was I informed
about this?"

"You know—moving the documentation process
to an online delivery system. I have done a

thorough analysis, gotten three quotes, and am putting the finishing touches on my 15-page summary report."

I'm sure you've guessed by now that, once we checked with the CIO, there was no new project. He'd casually asked a quiet question that my eager associate heard as a thundering demand for research. Given that he was satisfied with a simple "no," Pat certainly processed the question far beyond the standard required by the customer.

Sadly, it's not unusual for well-intentioned team members to go a little too far in response to the off-handed remark of someone in upper management. Another good friend told me that while he was serving as the Chief Engineer at a refinery in Texas, they were waiting for an executive visit. Someone noticed that several maintenance guys were outside spraying green paint on the grass. Apparently, the last time the CEO visited was during a drought, and he commented that "the grass sure was brown."

Someone noted that, and was determined to have it fixed for this visit!

Non-Right First Time

Anyone who's had to deal with the "experts at HQ" will appreciate this example that was given to me by a colleague:

A few years ago, my father-in law Al was superintendent of the fleet for the Indianapolis branch of a national baking company. It was his job to ensure that all the delivery trucks were kept in good repair, always ready and able to move fresh bread and bakery goods quickly from the central bakery out to restaurants and grocery stores around the state.

He shared with me the sad story of the day that he and his team first loaded up a brand new semi-trailer that had been ordered by the experts at national headquarters. The new truck looked great—shiny, spotless, with the company

logo displayed proudly on all sides. The driver
backed the truck into the dock, and instantly
the loaders swarmed in and out, filling the
trailer with rack upon rack of bread, ready for
immediate delivery.

To everyone's horror, when the driver went to
close the trailer doors, it couldn't be done! The
floor of the now-filled trailer sagged lower than
the bottom edge of doors, so they couldn't seal.

Properly designed trailers actually bow up slightly
in the center when empty so that they are pushed
flat by the weight of their designated cargo. As
it turned out, whoever at headquarters created
the specifications for the new trailer forgot to
calculate the weight of the *bread* when the rolling
racks were fully loaded. As a result, instead of
being flat, the new trailer drooped in the middle.

The company could have avoiding wasting a lot of
time, money, and bread if the specs had just been
right the first time.

Under-Utilization of People

My lean mentor and friend Chris has always pointed out that, in most cases, while people are on the job, they go about doing their work and doing what they are told. Outside of the office, though, these very same people might be leaders or managers in their family, churches, PTAs, or sports teams. A company culture that doesn't see these people as potential contributors may surely be under-utilizing their talents. Waste is manifest when someone who has the potential to lead or drive activities is not given such a role.

> "The mind has exactly the same power as the hands: Not merely to grasp the world, but to change it."
>
> *Colin Wilson*

Even our choice of words and images can set a tone that minimizes the value of an individual. Consider that workers used to be referred to as *hands*—for example, "farm hands" or "all hands on deck." What about their brains?

The symbol that's been adopted to represent people in process mapping and plant layout software symbolizes an individual, viewed from above, with arms set in position to take care of the work that is to be done. As a worker, what's your reaction to seeing yourself portrayed this way when you study such a map?

While hands are, indeed, important, part of lean thinking is an expectation that everybody should be fully engaged, and that their thinking—not just their labor— is critical to success. I propose changing this global symbol to one that reflects the *minds and potential ideas* that every worker in any part of the company can contribute toward continuous improvement. How about a light bulb instead? Let's focus on ideas and how they shed light on ways things can be improved!

Everybody should be fully engaged, and that
their thinking—not just their labor— is critical to
success.

Mura

Muda's partner, *mura*, is briefly defined as
inconsistency. *Mura* can be described as a
situation where flow is not even and there
is variability in how the process steps are
synchronized with one another. Unbalanced
workloads and uneven flow tie up valuable
capacity in one or more steps. And that means
that capacity that *could* have been used in
another process was lost. Wasted.

During a recent visit to a component assembly plant in Mexico, our team noted that an unusually large number of people were needed to coordinate product demand information received from the customer. Based on our calculations, they were using about twice as many people as we would normally expect. Upon further analysis, we determined that the software being used at the Mexico location was not up-to-date, and this created lots of manual handling and re-handling of information. In the end, the workload on the downstream side of the supply chain was unbalanced by a lack of technology.

Muri

The third musketeer of waste, *muri*, relates to overburdening a single step in a process. In a more practical sense, it deals with non-value added activities that derive from doing unnecessary work. In the case of a production process: over-producing, over-processing, or reprocessing. The workload is increased on the process step, but no new value is being added.

Dumping too much information, piling ideas on top of each other, and dragging up issues that are not to the point are typical examples where *muri* affects the communication process. In any type of communication that is meant to create clear meaning in everyone's head, overburdening with information may contribute to poor execution or incomplete assignments.

So what do *mura* and *muri* look like in communication terms? I always think of the time when one of our largest customers called the CEO directly with a complaint. The CEO immediately called in all the top brass to discuss the situation, make sure that everyone was aware of the problem, and determine what steps were needed across the organization to stop the negative incidents once and for all.

We all showed up on time, laptops and cell phones in hand, eager to get things resolved. The discussion began, and the CEO methodically called on each director in turn to respond individually about how his or her area might have affected the situation.

Unfortunately, all the managers who did not have the floor at any given time were busily scrolling through emails or thumbing their cell phones, taking care of other "urgent" matters rather than listening attentively to their peers. Any opportunity for collaboration, shared understanding, or brainstorming was lost—key connections and causality links were never made. Even though physically present in the same room, the leaders and their departments remained isolated, and no one could see how everyone was contributing to the customer's problem.

Mura happened when the managers were not aligned during the meeting and, even more significantly, when they and their departments were not aligned in the way they interacted (or not) across the organization. As a result, the company and its customers had to suffer the consequences of processes and hand-offs not being executed consistently.

Eventually, a team of troubleshooters in the company kicked off a Five Whys analysis.

Not surprisingly, a key root cause was the fact that there were too many urgent and important projects happening with looming deadlines. People were overwhelmed and overburdened—including the managers who brought their laptops to the CEO's meeting.

A fine example of *muri*, wouldn't you say?

At this point, as a lean practitioner or promoter, you should already be seeing opportunities to root out muda *in your communication processes. Now that you've listened with lean ears and looked through lean lenses at how communication processes become clogged with* muda, *it's time to explore ways to apply lean thinking and techniques to eliminate the conversational muck. Who knows—with a little Lean Potion #9, you may become a lean alchemist, transmuting* muda *into gold!*

Hiding in Plain Sight: Value Stream Mapping

I confess, I have a weakness for watching police procedurals on TV. Putting together the clues, testing hypotheses, and generally trying to outwit the bad guys scratches my problem-solving itch. I particularly like how the best of these TV shows have integrated serious science into their crime scene investigations.

One very popular tool for the investigators is a chemical solution called Luminol. When sprayed over an area that contains trace amounts of blood, Luminol reacts with the hemoglobin and emits a blue glow in a darkened room. Viola! What was invisible is now visible, and the authorities can spring into action.

In my mind, Lean Potion #9 is a lot like Luminol—it reveals process problems that are hiding in plain sight, allowing lean practitioners to spring into action.

Value Stream Mapping (VSM) is an apt example of a lean tool that excels at bringing hidden problems to light. The use of VSM became quite popular thanks, in part, to the book *Learning to See: Value Stream Mapping to Add Value and Eliminate* Muda, by Mike Rother and John

Shook. It describes in detail how you can use standard symbols to map out information and materials flows, and determine how value is being added...or not.

While working at a Tier 2 automotive supplier, I was involved in a project to improve collaboration with a key customer of ours. The perception on both sides was that too many orders were out of standard, which created two very costly situations:

Lean Lingo

Value Stream Mapping is a lean tool that employs a flow diagram documenting in high detail every step of a process. Many lean practitioners see value stream mapping as the fundamental tool to identify waste, reduce process cycle times, and implement process improvement.

from ASQ.org

(1) a large number of delivery problems that affected the production lines, and (2) the number of personnel on both sides that had to be available at all times to manage the situation.

Working in collaboration with our customer, we agreed that the first logical step was to draw a VSM to see where any waste might be lurking in our supply chain process. We covered a wall with chart paper, and kicked off the exercise with a joint team made up of lean practitioners, consultants, logistics staff, and operations personnel.

Pretty early in the mapping process, the source of the whole situation came to light as the lines and symbols for the signal sent to the supplier were drawn. As I recall, there were 16 different demand signals being sent to us by the customer. Requests came flooding in via emails, spreadsheets, web-based platforms, phone calls, and even snail-mail. All these signals created duplication, confusion, over-processing of information, unnecessary changeovers, excess inventory and…well, you get the picture.

Remember, a lean manufacturing process or a service does not start on its own. It is initiated and driven by a signal from the customer. In this case,

too many signals from the customer created *muda*
from the beginning—the production processes
stood no chance of succeeding. But until the
incoming signal stream was analyzed via VSM,
the Production group took the blame for being
the root cause of the delivery issues.

From a communication process perspective,
the real solution has to start on the customer
side. Why did they need 16 different signals?
What's the best way for the idea in a customer's
mind to be transmitted clearly and accurately
to all the other stakeholders in order for correct
action to happen?

> A lean manufacturing process or a service does
> not start on its own. It is initiated and driven by a
> signal from the customer.

All of this needs to be solved *before* attempting
to resolve any downstream issues. It might even
make sense to create a rating and metric for the
accuracy and clarity of the signal being received,

and how it aligns with the actual performance and execution to the expected demand.

My fundamental premise is that for adequate *execution* to occur, organizations need clean, lean *communication* processes happening between people at every level and in every link of the supply chain. As you will see, Value Stream Mapping is just the first of many lean tools that bring their magic to Lean Potion #9 to help you achieve efficient, effective communication.

Now that value-stream mapping has highlighted where value is being added in your communication processes, it's time to pour on the Lean Potion #9 to wash away any muda *that's been revealed. That brings us to the next essential lean discipline: the famous Five S's.*

It's all about *Flow*: Five S

In 2004, I had an opportunity to meet Mr. Masaki Imai, the world-famous author of *Kaizen* and *Gemba Kaizen*. In our chat, he asked me if I knew and understood the lean concept of Five S, to

which I modestly replied, "Yes, of course! Setting
things in order and keeping things clean."

> ## Lean Lingo
>
> **Five S programs** comprise a series of activities
> for eliminating wastes that contribute to errors,
> defects, and injuries:
> * Sort/*Seiri*—sort through items and keep
>   only what is needed (dispose of the rest)
> * Straighten/*Seiton*—"A place for everything
>   and everything in its place"
> * Shine/*Seiso*—cleaning as a form of
>   inspection that exposes abnormal and
>   pre-failure conditions that could hurt quality
> * Standardize/*Seiketsu*—develop systems and
>   procedures to maintain the first three Ss
> * Sustain/*Shitsuke*—maintain the
>   now-stabilized workplace through an
>   ongoing process of continuous improvement

Mr. Imai rolled his eyes, shook his head, and with
a laugh responded, "No, no, no—you guys just
don't get it. It is all about seeing the flow... and
making it shorter."

Now that we agree that communication is a
process, we can also agree that it has a flow.

We can further agree that in most work environments, even lean ones, it is rare to see people addressing communications issues from a *process* perspective. It certainly isn't taught in schools that way, either. So it's up to us, the bold advocates of Lean Potion #9 to bring process thinking to the realm of human-to-human communication and try to improve the process so that we can have a more efficient workplace.

The concept of *flow* is a key element of the lean mindset, a fundamental recipe for making production processes as efficient as possible. Also, flow helps us see things that would otherwise be hidden. As the eye grows accustomed to the way things move in a regular way, anything irregular sticks out like a sore thumb—just part of the beauty of this elegant system and philosophy of Five S.

The Five S methodology incorporates five specific concepts that originally were intended for shop floor and manufacturing activities with the idea of reducing the clutter in the environment so that things could be actually observed and orderly to determine their relevance and need.

Sort/*Seiri*

The first S is called *Sort* in English; the Japanese call it *Seiri*. Whatever you call it, S #1 is all about separating the necessary from the unnecessary. Keeping only what is essential and adds value to the work being done. Anything that isn't needed and doesn't add value to the process at hand should be discarded or removed.

Seiri begins with observation—putting on your lean lenses and looking closely, so you can bring to the surface those things that previously were not seen, yet were somehow creating waste. At a workstation, this could be wasted space taken up by an unused item, or perhaps the waste of creating an opportunity for an operator to use non-standard, outdated items and thereby create quality issues.

So how can we apply this concept to the process of communication?

Remember Shelby the Sender and Robin the Receiver? Communication is effective and adds value when the resulting idea in the receiver's mind matches the original idea created in the mind of the sender. The shared idea creates alignment, and any resulting actions and execution by the receiver(s) should meet the expectations of the sender—no variance! *Seiri* suggests several approaches that the sender and receiver can use to maximize the matching:

- Keep to the issue
- Sort out the noise
- Sort the urgent from the important
- Uncover underlying assumptions and opinions
- Root out deletion, distortion, and generalizations
- Set aside authority and hierarchy

Keep to the Issue

If we define *issue* as being the "task at hand," then we can agree that anything in the communication process that we identify as "not needed to achieve the task at hand" should be removed.

Seiri keeps us focused on the issue, so we can recognize any deviation from it in a conversation or other communication and get back on track. This avoids wasted time and discussions not related to what the communication *should* be about. Something as simple as jotting down side issues and deferring discussion on them until later can help keep everyone on topic. (You may have seen professional facilitators use this trick, often called a Parking Lot, to keep sessions on track.)

Sort out the Noise

As the earlier *muda* examples have shown, communication attempts can contain non-value-add junk that interferes with the effective transmission and reception of the message.

Communications experts refer to anything that blocks successful communication as *noise*. Here are some typical examples of noise to eliminate:

- *Physical noise* or *external noise*—environmental distractions, such as poorly heated rooms, startling sounds, distracting graphics, loud sounds or music, or someone talking near you.

- *Physiological noise*—biological influences that distract you from communicating competently, such as feeling sick, being exhausted, being really hungry, or being in pain.

- *Psychological noise*—preconceptions, biases, and assumptions, such as thinking that someone who speaks with a Southern accent is dumb, or that someone from a foreign country who can't speak English well needs for you to speak loudly and slowly to them.

- *Semantic noise*—word choices that are confusing and distracting, such as using jargon or unnecessarily showing off a large vocabulary. Similarly, using compound/complex, convoluted sentences, or odd syntax also create confusion.

Sort the Urgent from the Important

In his Habit #3, "Put First Things First,"[9] Stephen R. Covey masterfully explores the challenge we all face in prioritizing our energy and our time. Should I focus on the urgent items that are clamoring for my attention*right now?* Or should I invest in those things that have deeper, long-term value, but don't necessarily have to be addressed at the moment?

In struggling with this dilemma, *seiri* can be a powerful ally. Trying to tackle too many issues at once creates an opportunity for *muri.* Things tend to go unresolved for long periods of time because resources might be focused on different tasks, all of which are, in fact, important. Urgent matters might also suffer from a lack

---

[9] From *The 7 Habits of Highly Effective People®*

of proper analysis and solution because of the
crunch for time and a similar dispersion of
resources.

Aligning your resources can improve the process of
taking care of issues when the urgent is sorted from
the important, and more clear communication is
provided to all stakeholders, insofar as expected due
dates, critical paths, and so forth.

Uncover Underlying Assumptions and Opinions

The twenty-first century workplace routinely
throws together people from different cities,
different countries, different education, different
generations, and different backgrounds. People
bringing diverse cultures and experiences
to the table also tend to bring with them
assumptions through which they think and
operate. This makes it difficult to communicate
and obtain shared meaning, because each
discussion involves a hodge-podge of different
assumptions and opinions.

Because many of those opinions are ingrained in
our experiences and are fundamental to the way
we think as individuals, we are often not aware
of the effect they have in dialogue with others,
who also listen and talk through the filters of
their assumptions. Because the assumptions or
opinions are deeply embedded in our minds, we
tend to defend them without even questioning
them. When you've got multiple people operating
from diverse assumptions, judgments and
misunderstandings between team members are
almost inevitable.

Seiri in this context can be used to challenge a
team and its members to recognize and bring
to the surface all the underlying, unquestioned
assumptions that are filtering both inbound and
outbound communications. The initial goal is *not*
to discredit or judge the assumptions, but simply
to take an inventory of them.

As the process continues, each assumption can
be compared with observable data and factual
information to determine whether or not it is

valid. By approaching underlying assumptions and opinions in this way, participants tend to be more open to sharing opinions without being defensive and creating animosity. This opens up the possibility of *truly* listening to others and understanding *their* frame of mind and point of view.

Another form of assumption is a simplistic faith that people, processes, and technology always work the way they are *supposed* to. Remember the Airbus A380 debacle? One writer noted, "In theory, the fact that the design centers were sharing their drawings meant that the electrical system designed in Germany would be compatible with the airframe components designed in France."

The operative word here is *theory*. That assumption proved to be incorrect and very costly.

All too often, things are different in practice. Sorting out these disconnects isn't difficult, but it does require attention and a willingness to perform reality checks regularly. Ask your colleagues for confirmation. Test your processes and technologies

to know how they really work. As Ronald Reagan
famously said, "Trust, but verify."

Root Out Deletion, Distortion, and Generalization

With *seiri* in mind as your tool, you can stay alert
at all times during group interactions and try to
bring to the surface any deletions, distortions,
and generalizations that might be confusing
communications and thwarting alignment. Each
of these three meaning-warpers can contribute to
miscommunication and have a negative effect on
the shared meaning we are trying to achieve.

Deletion

Sometimes it's what's *not* there that creates the
problems. For example, several years ago, my
company agreed to help a new client deliver
a mission-critical project. We *and* they were
confident that we were experts who could pull
off this implementation without a hitch. We
hired some new engineers, trained them on our

standard work process, and got them started on the project.

A few weeks into the implementation, our CEO got a frantic call from our client's top brass, screaming that the new engineers were incompetent and had *no* idea what they were doing. What happened to our alleged expertise and ability to implement?

As it turned out, although lean had been widely implemented on our shop floor, some of the product know-how and "secret formulas" were not baked into the standard work documentation. For whatever reasons, the engineers who had originally set up the process failed to fully document the details, and when they left the company, they took their institutional knowledge with them, leaving us and our clients in the lurch. Critical information had been left out—*deleted*.

When specific details or data are omitted—deliberately or not—from a conversation or presentation, that deletion has a potentially dire influence on the outcome and actions that the team will undertake. If deletions can be uncovered and labeled as such during the communication process, those gaps can be addressed and the process corrected before confusion or failure occur.

Waste can be expected wherever decisions are made and actions are taken as a result of a team dialogue where details have been deleted or omitted. This incomplete exchange of ideas can result in unexpected costs and are a prime opportunity for the use of *seiri* in identifying a potential cause for *muda*.

When we conducted root cause analysis sessions about the lost institutional knowledge issue, we recognized that was vital to have *all* of the functional areas represented in the meetings. Every session demonstrated anew that the engineers saw things one way while the operators saw things differently. Each group "deleted" facts based on their specific point of view. Some things were so obvious to them that they never realized

those details were worth mentioning, which,
naturally, left anyone from *outside* the group with
a gap in their understanding. The complete, true
situation could be constructed *only* when all the
participants provided their comprehensive version,
with all assumptions noted.

I recently took a three-day Operational
Excellence workshop presented at Performance
Solutions by Milliken. One central part of their
philosophy relates to our point about deletion. It's
called Zero-Loss Thinking[10], which asserts that
typical budgetary approaches allow some wastes
and take them for granted.

Zero-Loss Thinking creates an environment
where *nothing* is taken for granted; instead,
everything must be considered an opportunity
for improvement. It challenges the team to view
things from "what is possible" and not from
"what exists." It highlights the total of the losses.
This methodology sets off a different process

[10] To learn more about Zero-Loss Thinking, read http://www.
performancesolutionsbymilliken.com/en-us/Documents/The-Systematic-
Approach-to-Operational-Excellence.pdf.

improvement direction that considers not only the traditional wastes, but also any possible waste that was previously "deleted" from the scope.

Distortion

The case for distortion is similar to the case for deletion, and can also happen deliberately or not. Distortion in communication takes many forms and can appear any time people are trying to convey messages and achieve agreement. Need to see some examples? The next time you tune in to dueling political commentators chewing over any polarizing issue, be on the lookout for these classic distortion techniques:

- Selective use of facts—presenting only the facts that my side agrees with while ignoring any that disagree or offer an alternative perspective

- Oversimplification—streamlining complex issues so much that critical nuances are lost; sometimes takes the form of using an

incomplete analogy or a vague metaphor
to help neophytes grasp the essence of a
multidimensional situation without ever
going back to fill in the details

- Unequal attention—paying extra attention
  to issues my side cares about while
  shortchanging other, objectively equal issues
- Ad hominem—attacking people or
  personalities on irrelevant points instead of
  addressing the real issues at hand
- Misleading statistics—using data and
  results of quantitative analysis without
  fully understanding them or confirming
  their validity

Distortions in the workplace are probably less
blatant, and can certainly creep in without
malicious intent; however, they are still potentially
harmful.

Careful review and preparation of information,
in addition to the use of *seiri* to detect the
opportunity of distorted details, will be very useful

in avoiding potential *muda*. Every team member
should feel comfortable, even encouraged,
to respectfully challenge details during any
conversation, with the goal of identifying
and avoiding unwanted costs associated with
distortion in all its forms.

Generalizations

The great eighteenth-century poet William Blake
might have been exaggerating a trifle when he said,
"To generalize is to be an idiot." But there's no doubt
that relying on generalizations *can* be risky. The
danger of generalizing in today's complex workplace,
of course, is that we might make big decisions or
form important opinions based on a limited number
of examples. Examples that may or may not actually
be germane to the issue. A generalization can lead
to waste when it slips into the information exchange
without being identified as such. It can affect the
outcome of a process in a negative way, where
critical details are not considered and a unique
situation might be misconstrued as a general one.

On a more personal level, generalizations can throw up barriers between people rather than build bridges. I vividly remember having to do damage control on the relationship between Alex, the Logistics manager at my assembly facility in Mexico, and the Finance manager at our headquarters in the US. Alex received a call from the Finance manager about a procedural error with some report. It seems that the Finance manager made a big point of insisting that *"you guys* down there [i.e., every manager in the Mexican location] *always* do this wrong!" Alex did not take kindly to that generalization. It felt more like an accusation, with a tone that implied "us versus them," "losers," and "can't get anything right." In your conversations, sort out any words that generalize in absolutes, such as *always* and *never.* And be sure you know exactly who "you guys" are before you speak, lest you suggest meanings that might be received in a negative way.

As you look for deletions, distortions, and generalizations, remember to look beyond just the local, internal problem areas, and consider that these issues can infest communication processes at every level, up to and including global supply chains. The big picture deletions, distortions, and generalizations should be sorted out in a way that enables everyone to better find and remove the waste.

Members of Alcoholics Anonymous are frequently reminded that one must accept and acknowledge that he or she is an alcoholic. Only then can change and healing begin. In our case, the first step is accepting that the current communication processes across the supply chain may not be the best, and that there is waste present that needs be reduced or removed. *Seiri* can help you sort those out and separate them from the meat of the message that you are trying to convey.

Set Aside Hierarchy and Authority

Picture yourself in a big meeting where a mix of managers, directors, and even VPs are all there together, listening to a presentation about a vital issue your company needs to address. Finally, after laying out several courses of action, the presenter says, "Okay, now that you've heard the options, what do you think?"

The room falls silent, and everybody stares at the notes in their lap, studiously avoiding making eye contact with the presenter. "What are they all waiting for?" you may think.

They are waiting for the HiPPO—the **Hi**ghest **P**aid **P**erson's **O**pinion.

All too often, organizations let job title, hierarchical position, and authority dominate the communication process. If the goal of our communication effort is to ensure that everyone at every level shares the clearest, most reliable information without assumptions, preconditions, and pressures, then **everyone** needs to share equally in sorting out the necessary from the unnecessary, the truth from the assumptions. This means that leaders have to make it safe for all players, regardless of title or tenure, to ask hard questions and separate the wheat from the chaff.

In summary...

As you brew up a batch of Lean Potion #9 to sprinkle on your own organization's conversations, remember to use *seiri* to sort the necessary from the unnecessary by:

- Keeping to the issue
- Sorting out the noise
- Sorting the urgent from the important
- Uncovering underlying assumptions and opinions
- Rooting out deletion, distortion, and generalizations
- Setting aside authority and hierarchy

Our next stop on the Five S tour is *seiton*—set in order.

Set in Order/*Seiton*

Did you know that the lean concept of *seiton* was popularized by an American minister in the early 1800's and was the topic of books of that era targeting sailors and homemakers? Of course back then, the concept was communicated as "a place for everything, and everything in its place."

Regardless of who thought of it first, *seiton* is another lean tool that makes a seamless transition into the new challenge of improving the productivity and effectiveness of our communication processes.

> Knowledge workers need to have their information resources at their fingertips just as surely as assembly line workers need their air wrenches and shop rags within easy reach.

On the shop floor, *setting things in order* means organizing the work **area** so that everything needed for adding value in a production operation is always in the same place, as close as possible to where it is actually used, and clearly labeled. Conversely, anything that doesn't add value is moved away from the work area.

In much the same way, *setting things in order* for effective communication means organizing the work **day** so that time, attention, and energy are all focused on adding value for the customer. We can use this second step of the Five S system to drive awareness and focus on *value-added* discussions and dialogues. If you see any communication component that doesn't add value, you should tag it, bag it, and drag it away!

Let's consider five ways you can set things in order for successful communication:

- Focus on the customer
- Manage intellectual capital
- Set a tone of curiosity and discovery
- Facilitate functional interdependence
- Clarify how decisions are made

Focus on the Customer

People form companies to serve customers by providing them with products and services to fulfill their needs. Savvy lean leaders know that everything their business does begins and ends with:

- Understanding what customers want, need, and value—what will thrill them
- Knowing how the business satisfies the customer
- Improving the effectiveness of how the business satisfies the customer[11]

Whether interactions occur within the organization or with entities outside of the organization, communication adds value to the degree that it moves the company forward toward delivering what the customer needs and wants. Deviating from this original intent often leads to misunderstandings and a greater focus on internal politics and personal problems, which definitely add no value. In settings where cross-cultural issues frequently create misunderstandings, redirecting attention to the customer's needs helps everyone rise above any petty squabbling.

This is a good time to pause and remember that your efforts to focus on the customer mustn't

[11] Lean leader bullets quoted from http://www.dummies.com/how-to/content/lean-for-dummies-cheat-sheet.html.

overlook your *internal* customers. Anyone, inside or outside the company, who receives the results of your work is your customer. Internal customers are colleagues who deserve our best efforts at ensuring they receive complete, accurate, and clear details as participants in a supply chain of information.

Consider this example of non-value-added communication from my days at our lock and hardware plant. A key customer was waiting for us to ramp up production on a new part. At one point, we needed to build some samples to use as prototypes for a mock lean production line.

Carlos, the engineer in charge, was quite ambiguous in his instructions to the operators. Instead of providing them with written specifications or detailed drawings of the parts, he just gave them vague statements on how the parts should look and how they were going to be used by the customer.

The operators were irked and frustrated. Rather than adding value for the customer by creating useful prototypes, their time, materials, and patience were wasted on trying to guess what Carlos had in mind. They were not able to perform because they didn't have enough information.

Needless to say, the resulting parts were not usable, and I had to step in to provide the operators with usable plans. The end customer was not pleased because so much time was lost to rework. And I certainly was not pleased on any level—lack of effective communication resulted in a hit to my bottom line.

Your customers—internal and external—are *always* the final judge of whether your product satisfies them 100%. Clearly, Carlos's inadequate communication attempts did not add value for anyone. Set things in order—make it all about your customer and how you are adding value for them!

Manage your Intellectual Capital

We've talked about communication being the process by which human beings share

ideas with each other—how they exchange
meaning and messages, and how they establish
agreements. This accumulated body of meanings
and messages and agreements might be called
knowledge. It might even be termed *intellectual
capital*, as explained at length in Thomas A.
Stewart's book, *Intellectual Capital: the New
Wealth of Nations*. According to Stewart:

> Every organization houses valuable
> intellectual materials in the form of assets
> and resources, tacit and explicit perspectives,
> and capabilities, data, information,
> knowledge, and maybe wisdom.

Where would you find your organization's
intellectual capital? Well, some of it is in the
minds of the people who work there—human
capital. Some of it resides in the structures of
the organization, like documents, processes,
computer systems, training programs, and
such—structural capital. And your customers and
your relationships and reputation with them are
also considered intellectual capital.

Think for a moment about how you'd find the answer to a customer's question if it wasn't something you knew off the top of your head. Do you see yourself pawing through piles of papers, flailing through file folders, or tensely typing search words into your intranet or database system? Would you wander through the building, asking experts on the hoof? And once you find what you think the answer is...how can you be sure? Is this the most correct, current, and complete info?

If that accurately describes your situation, your intellectual capital clearly needs a gallon or two of Lean Potion #9 to set it in order. Knowledge workers need to have their information resources at their fingertips just as surely as assembly line workers need their air wrenches and shop rags within easy reach.

Remember, too, that we've defined communication conversations to include *every* channel, not just individuals talking face to face. "Conversations" can take place over vast spans of time or distance as ideas are exchanged via scrolls,

books, electronic knowledge management systems,
and whatever comes next.

To implement *seiton* fully is to set in order *all*
information, no matter where and how it's stored,
and to ensure that all individuals have access to
what they need. Training classes, documents, and
databases are all structural capital that adds value
by making sure everyone in the value chain knows
what they need to know.

Some companies even implement central
document control systems or knowledge
management systems. Whether manual or
automated, these systems are intended to keep the
most current, correct, and complete information
readily accessible, while also managing archives of
obsolete information, in case it is ever needed for
lessons-learned or historical perspective. Of course,
any such system is only as good as the processes
used to maintain it and the people who manage it.

Adopting a good *seiton* mindset for
information storage and flow will help keep

non-value-add situations away from your
intellectual capital.

Set a Tone of Curiosity and Discovery

To foster lean communication, leaders must
establish an environment of trust, a culture where
curiosity and discovery are promoted as useful
tools for illuminating problems and finding
solutions—both of which add enormous value.

This tone of welcoming curiosity and creativity
in communication leads to a self-fulfilling
cycle of collaboration and cooperation among
all stakeholders inside and outside of the
organization. More people begin to participate,
and fewer keep silent out of fear. Chastising,
criticizing, and punishing people for "sounding
dumb" is certainly a non-value-add activity, and by
this point, should have been taken care of via the
seiri phase by finding and removing such behavior.

Here's a practical step to get you started.
At the start of a meeting or discussion,

state that bringing in new ideas and asking thought-provoking questions is encouraged, no matter how "far out" they might seem. You will probably find that you end up with more ideas, and that those ideas are more innovative. You now have more possibilities that you can push through the familiar Plan-Do-Check-Act cycle to test objectively, refine, and eventually build upon.

Facilitate Functional Interdependence

An effective and efficient organizational structure is one where value is added with every interaction that happens between the various functional areas and departments. Do handoffs in your organization reliably add value, or do critical messages and actions get lost while trying to navigate the gaps between silos?

Seiton tells us to set in order the way in which these interactions actually take place by having a reliable, repeatable process for managing interdependencies. Each team, department, division, or supplier must have a crystal clear understanding of its own mission, vision, and principles. And they must further understand how they and their mission/vision/principles link up with all the other entities cross-organizationally to the benefit of the customer. Ultimately, the goal (and the challenge) is to align expectations along the entire length of the supply chain, with every handoff—internal and external—adding value. Anything less, and you are simply driving waste into the communication processes.

Clarify How Decisions are Made

Getting to a decision is often a process with numerous non-value-added steps. Just the wait-time added by review and approval steps adds mucho *muda*. Does your organization have agreed-upon, well-documented guidelines for who is responsible for making which decisions, what process should be used, who should participate, and what inputs will be relevant to getting to a decision?

When decision-making is set in order, guiding principles are established and taught to every

associate, creating a value-added route for
questions to follow. For example, implementing a
basic RACI
matrix[12] can go a
long way toward
making sure that
all the right
people and *only*
the right people
are pulled into the
decision path.

Lean Lingo

RACI matrix:
specifies for various
decisions which
individuals or entities
are **R**esponsible,
Accountable,
Consulted, or **I**nformed.

In summary...

As you've seen, the second S can be a potent
potion for bringing order to the chaos of some
communication processes. Make sure every
batch of Lean Potion #9 sets things in order by:

- Focusing on the customer
- Managing intellectual capital
- Setting a tone of curiosity and discovery

[12] For more about RACI matrices, read http://asq.org/service/body-of-knowledge/tools-RASIC-RACI.

- Facilitating functional interdependence
- Clarifying how decisions are made

You've sorted. You've set in order. Now is your chance to shine!

Shine/*Seiso*

Seiso shines the lean spotlight on the need to keep things clean. One of my colleagues told me about her first experience seeing *seiso* in action:

On a visit to the Columbus, Ohio area in the mid-1980s, my husband and I had an opportunity to tour the headquarters of TruSports Racing, home of Indianapolis 500 Champion Bobby Rahal and his team. The tour group walked through the office building and admired the jam-packed trophy room. Then we were invited to step into the garage area.

Now, I've spent some time around the local gas station garage, so I expected to see the usual grungy walls and greasy floor, with every surface covered in a layer of oil, dust, and goodness-knows-what, along with workbenches and rolling tool chests cluttered with sockets, screw drivers, wrenches, and rags.

I was completely blown away when I stepped through the garage door into a spotless, spacious work area that *literally* shined with stainless steel cabinets, an immaculate polished floor, gigantic windows, and blazing overhead lights. It looked like an operating room for race cars. And indeed, that's what it was.

The crew chief and all the mechanics were fully committed to *seiso*, whether they knew it by that name that or not. And it makes sense. Even then, Indy-style race cars were just low-flying airplanes, with every mechanical part honed to the tightest of tolerances for maximum performance. One speck of dust in the wrong place, and your race day could end abruptly, even tragically.

Is your communication process honed for maximum performance?

As you know from bringing *seiso* into your own shop, a clean work area is essential for any production process to be efficient. First, a dirty area conveys, in a non-verbal way, an absence of control, commitment, and caring. Further, a lack of cleanliness can create production shut-downs, quality problems, and, worst of all, accidents that can injure people.

Cleaning up a work area dramatically reveals the true surfaces and state of the equipment, allowing you to identify and address potential points of failure *before* they create big problems. And cleaning does not mean just dusting off things and removing excess lubricants or dirt from machinery and equipment.

Cleaning implies leaving things as they were *before* you started the process. This is the context we will use for analyzing how *seiso* can be useful in burnishing our communication processes. For our purposes, *seiso* in communication includes three components:

- Restore things to their original state
- Build rapport
- Clarify the issues

Restore Things to their Original State

When my children were young, they were not thrilled about doing their kitchen chores. "Why do we have to wash and dry the dishes and put them in the cabinet every single night, Dad?" they whined. "Because if you leave them dirty," I replied, "what are you going to put your food on for the next meal?"

The logic of restoring things to their original state is supremely clear in the kitchen. So why not extend that reasoning to the boardroom?

A meeting is over and the conversation has ended. Now things need to be restored to their original state, and I'm not just talking about the chairs and the coffee cups.

If a meeting has generated a certain amount of misunderstanding or ill-feeling among team members, and it ends without anyone cleaning up the mess left behind, the effectiveness of the communication from that meeting and in future interactions may be quite low.

Restoring to the original state means clearly summarizing the what, where, when, who, why, and how, and reflecting back for confirmation until clarity is absolute for all. It also means that when personal issues arise during the communication process, they must be promptly and appropriately addressed. Leaving a breach of trust or an insult unrepaired is like leaving an open wound unattended. Things will fester, creating problems now and in the future. Misunderstandings can linger for a long time, and the friction they cause is simply non-value-added waste.

> "...an apology can show strength of character, demonstrate emotional competence, and reaffirm that both parties share values in their relationship they want to commit to."

An apology and clarification serve here as a good practice of *seiso* in the communication process. Apologies can be quite powerful. The United Nations website actually has a page devoted to how to offer and how to receive apologies appropriately. As noted there, "An apology can show strength of character, demonstrate emotional competence, and reaffirm that both parties share values in their relationship they want to commit to."[13]

Once something has been said or conveyed outright, the message has been noted and received by someone. There is no going back. The only thing to be done is to clarify or apologize. In this sense, this is a *corrective*action to return things to a more positive state. It is also a *preventative* action that should fend off any further negative consequences. Finally, it's also a great opportunity to understand what went wrong in this process and apply it as a lessons-learned in future interactions.

Build Rapport

For mechanical devices, grit in the gears is a serious problem, because of the friction and damage it creates where the gears engage. People, too, can experience friction as they try to

---

[13] To read more about apologies, go to https://www.un.org/en/ombudsman/apologies.shtml.

engage with each other. *Seiso* for interpersonal relationships is all about cleaning out any points of friction and misunderstanding, so that the parties involved can begin to build rapport.

> Rapport—a close and harmonious relationship in which the people or groups concerned understand each other's feelings or ideas and communicate well; relation marked by harmony, conformity, accord, or affinity.

Building rapport is a *process*—typically an iterative one that involves listening, learning, and engaging, not unlike lean's familiar plan-do-check-act cycle.

Rapport is also a *state* where two or more individuals have achieved significant trust, harmony, and sensitivity to each other's thoughts and feelings. Typically, people who share rapport deeply understand each other and can have very effective conversations. They rarely suffer from variance as they exchange information back and forth, and when variances do occur, they are comfortable with raising and resolving the issue.

Once reached, rapport builds on itself and creates ever-deepening trust and commitment. It's the ideal basis for an effective team.

In the best lean teams, everyone is responsible for maintaining *seiso*. Rather than perceiving clean-up tasks as low-value, low-status work, these activities are appreciated as an essential part of keeping the entire enterprise humming and the customers delighted. When all hands pitch in to bring on the shine, the sense of working as a team to complete an overall objective is enhanced. Likewise, as noted earlier, everyone involved in a communication process should feel proud to contribute to pointing out and eliminating any "grit in the gears" they find.

Clarify the Issues

Have you ever been listening to someone chatter on and on about a situation and muttered to yourself, "Well, that's about as clear as mud." Sometimes ideas become encrusted with unnecessary layers of meaning. Unneeded complexity creeps in. Unfamiliar terminology disguises a perfectly obvious point. And the conversation goes in circles without ever conveying clear meaning.

Just as lean experts clean an assembly line, you can remove the mud (and *muda*) from the surface of a conversation by being attentive, asking good questions, and using feedback loops to confirm understanding. In a well-shined conversation, each participant strives to clearly state the points that are being discussed. *Seiso* also implies stating clearly what the point is *not*. When everyone has absolute clarity about the issues being considered, the conversation can flow briskly from Point A to Point B without wandering and wasting valuable time.

Do you remember my colleague and her team member, Pat? Here's a story that highlights the need to clarify issues and remove semantic roadblocks:

Pat and I worked together on an ad hoc Process Improvement Team (PIT) with folks from a different division, trying to standardize our project management processes. We were getting very close to an agreement.

One Tuesday, we were scheduled to have a
meeting. I couldn't attend, but I was confident
that Pat could handle things and wrap up
the PIT. When we got together later that
afternoon, I asked her how things turned
out. "Oh, it was awful!" she said. "Discussions
broke down completely. We may have to start
all over."

The next day, I called an emergency meeting
of the PIT to see what went wrong. After we
assembled, I asked Harper, from the other
division, to bring me up to date on the problem.

"Well, we believe strongly that we need to have
project templates, but *you* guys keep saying we
need to use boilerplates. We argued about it for 45
minutes yesterday."

"Pat, is that true?"

"Yes, it is. Everything I've read stresses that having
boilerplates is essential, and I believe we need to
go that route."

So, Harper—can you tell me what a template is?"

"Sure! It's a robust reusable work breakdown structure that can be customized for individual projects."

"Okay, Pat. Now tell me what a boilerplate is."

"Um…it's a robust reusable work breakdown structure that can be customized for individual projects."

We wrapped things up pretty quickly after that!

Consider all the *muda* that was generated because nobody asked the right questions to clean up the misunderstanding created by a simple semantic difference.

By stating clearly what you mean, defining the real purpose of discussion, and staying focused on it, any underlying agendas, individual goals, and confusion can be removed from the conversation just as you would scrub away dirt and unwanted debris from a workbench.

In summary...

Just to be perfectly clear, remember these steps
when you use Lean Potion #9 as the super solvent
for shining your communication processes:

- Restore things to their original state
- Build rapport
- Clarify the issues

By this point, you've made great strides toward
mucking out the *muda* from your conversations.
As always on the Five S pilgrimage, the next stop
is *seiketsu*—develop systems and procedures to
maintain the first three Ss.

Standardize/*Seiketsu*

Long before the Toyota Production System
came into being, Henry Ford recognized the
value of standardization in manufacturing.
All Model T's were identical, made of
interchangeable parts, and available "in any color
you like, as long as it's black." Then, as now, a

standard process allowed greater productivity, quality, and consistency.

Today's lean manufacturing disciples call it *seiketsu*, and they have taken the essence of standardization to an exponentially higher level. Still, the basics remain the same: a production process is set up with clear steps and instructions showing how to perform each operation in a way that ensures a repeatable, specific outcome. As each iteration of the process yields its output, that output is compared to an explicit, measurable model that defines the ideal expected output; i.e., The Standard.

Seiketsu typically focuses on standardizing the Five S process, but expanding our use of *seiketsu* is also essential. Obtaining universal agreement on the standard creates a benchmark to which you can always return whenever you need to confirm, to calibrate, and to set the next bar for continuous improvement.

When an organization makes sure that every process step is executed the same way under the same conditions every time, its outputs are much more likely to conform to The Standard the majority of the time. As a lean practitioner, you routinely verify that outputs meet The Standard, and when they don't, you address the variance appropriately. Sometimes that means improving the process. Sometimes it even means adopting a new standard. All of this is part and parcel of the classic Five S system and the PDCA cycle of continuous improvement we know and love.

Although it may initially sound odd, *seiketsu* can be applied to communication processes in at least three ways:

- Choose a common language
- Check for variance
- Establish clear agreements

Choose a Common Language

Your best chance of achieving consistent communication success comes from conversing with your audiences—especially customers—in their preferred language, using familiar words that they can relate to easily. I'm not just talking about English versus Farsi versus Japanese. I'm also talking about jargon, acronyms, and buzzwords that sometimes build barriers rather than transmit ideas.

In today's global, multicultural organizations, choosing the right base language is critical to success. Very often, English is the language of choice. And it's a great choice in some ways, because it is a syntactically flexible language, rich with synonyms and a vibrant, ever-expanding vocabulary. Those same characteristics make it a real bear[14] to master when English is not your native tongue. As we

> "When my associates and I studied Toyota's product development system, we found that **standardization promotes effective teamwork** by teaching employees similar **terminology**, skills, and rules of play."
>
> *From The* Toyota Way, *by Jeffrey K. Liker*

[14] Bear? Furry mammal of the family *Ursidae*? To carry? To tolerate? Metaphor for something tough to manage? Naked? (No, that's *bare*.)

saw earlier, choosing English as a shared working language didn't necessarily work all that well for the Airbus A380 team.

In the old days, IBM required its technical writers to compose manuals using only terms from a restricted list of English words, and then made sure that all members of their support staff in every country around the globe were fully trained in that limited vocabulary. If you are part of an international team, you might borrow that idea and create a standard project glossary for all to share. I've even known businesses to maintain a corporate glossary to help associates and other stakeholders decode acronyms, learn proprietary system names, and so forth, even when everyone spoke the same native language.

Beyond the basic challenge of sharing a common "surface-level" definition for words, languages also reflect the cultures in which they evolved. For example, one reason this book exists is because I believe that lean practitioners who share a common language and philosophy are uniquely positioned to lead change in our organizations with a goal of achieving more effective communication.

As you strive to streamline communication processes in your organization, selecting and standardizing on a common language is a monumental positive step toward preventing variance.

Check for Variance

When I convey a message to you, my goal is for you to have in *your* mind the same meaning that I had in *my* mind when I sent the message. In this communication process, the meaning in my mind is **The Standard**.

Do you remember Shelby the Sender and Robin the Receiver? Shelby wanted Robin

> **Lean Lingo**
>
> Standard—the explicit, measurable model that defines the ideal expected output

to draw a triangle, but Robin misunderstood the
message and drew a circle instead.

Shelby the Sender   Robin the Receiver

Clearly, a variance exists. If the standard
is *triangle*, then *circle* does not conform to
the standard. An outside observer of this
non-value-added communication process might
immediately recommend an improvement: Shelby
could choose more specific words. For example,
"Robin, draw a triangle."

Traditional efforts to improve communication—and
leadership—typically focus on the sender's
side. Use explicit language. Use the right
communication channels. Monitor outcomes to
confirm that the correct meaning was conveyed.
And that's all excellent advice. However, the
receiver role needs to be an active one, as well.

Communication starts with broadcasting the message, as a radio station might do. But broadcasting only works when a *receiver* is (a) turned on and (b) tuned to the right frequency. Even *then,* the broadcaster doesn't know if real communication has occurred. The final step in the communication cycle is the feedback loop. Somehow, the receiver needs to let the broadcaster know that *a* message was received, and together, they need to determine if the *correct* message was received.

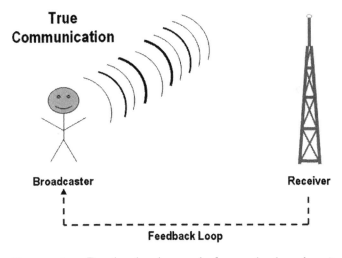

True Communication

Broadcaster

Receiver

Feedback Loop

Remember Raphael, who took down the breakers? The whole misunderstanding could have been avoided by simply asking him to tell us exactly what he was planning to do in response to our request.

That last step—determining if the **correct** message was received—is the *seiketsu* moment, checking the process outcome against The Standard. And if you find a variance, lean practice tells you it's time to troubleshoot. Break out the Five Whys, the Ishikawa Diagrams, and the Pareto Charts, because it's time to root out the root cause!

Don't kid yourself. Even when a team has made a good faith effort to establish a standard language and standard broadcasting methods (e.g., speaking, writing, texting, emailing, online repositories, printed documents, to name only a few), variance can still happen.

> **Lean Lingo**
>
> ***Pareto Chart*—**
> graphical tool for identifying the 20% of the issues that create 80% of the problems.

The receivers in the communication cycle must take ownership of their special role. Be engaged. Ask questions. Sort out noise. Reflect back what you *think* you heard to be **sure** you received the correct message (*seiketsu*). In short, become an *active* listener.[15]

The sender and the receiver share equal responsibility for making sure that messages are exchanged without variance. It's all about achieving *clarity*. Sadly, it is not uncommon for any of us to blithely take action on a request from a boss or a customer, only to get to an outcome that does not meet expectations. This not only points out a lack of clarity between the parties, but it also exposes the lack of a standard for two or more parties to accept the shared meaning and full understanding of an expectation.

This is what agreements are all about, and is the third element of our work with *seiketsu*, which

---

[15] Much has been written about active listening and other listening styles. For an excellent overview, download http://www.mindtools.com/CommSkll/Mind%20Tools%20Listening.pdf.

contains the formula for standard work in the communication process.

Establish Clear Agreements

In the communication process, we can adopt the lean philosophy of standardized work by using *agreements*. The context here is not necessarily the legal sense of an agreement, although it does, in fact, get used in the legal arena in the very same way: when the performance requirements of an agreement are not met, all parties must come together to solve the perceived discrepancy between the *expected* result and the *actual* outcome.

Getting work done in a business environment usually means that several functional areas in the company have to come together and agree on the steps and activities required to achieve the specific outcome needed by the customer.

> Answer the burning questions of (a) who is going to do what by when, (b) why, how, and where are they doing it, and (c) what if something goes wrong?

In some environments, deliberations leading to an agreement tend to be informal. This works in small teams or long-standing teams where natural cohesion, harmony, rapport, and experience working together allow for many successful outcomes.

Many environments, however, are becoming increasingly complex and multicultural. The prudent lean communicator can safely assume that, unless a process is in place to establish absolute clarity about expected outcomes, Murphy's Law and entropy will affect that outcome in an undesirable way.

> *Entropy*—nature tends to move from order to disorder in isolated systems

Seiketsu and the 6 + 1 Steps to Establishing Agreements

In lean lingo, *Standard Work* is a method for defining best practices in a process, and ensuring that everyone on the team is following them to reliably deliver the expected results. In a communication process, establishing agreements helps us get our needs met and maintain the relationships we need at work to execute complex activities. Agreements allow for a clear understanding of the goals and become the basis for determining what went wrong when the target condition is *not* met.

Agreements get their power from the level of clarity achieved by each individual player. Fulfill the agreement, and you know that the message being communicated is received and acknowledged by the receiver with an absolute understanding.

A classic standard work agreement in the communication process consists of 6 + 1 basic clauses that answer the burning questions of (a) who is going to do what by when, (b) why, how, and where are they doing it, and (c) what if something goes wrong? Let's consider each clause in some detail.

The *Who* Clause

Businesses move forward through the efforts of their people, so the *Who* clause must answer these questions:

- Who will execute the action?
- Who is responsible for overall coordination of the actions?
- Who among our stakeholders will be affected?
- Who will join us in doing things that move us toward the new target condition?

The *Who* clause goes back to the question of resources. Identify who will be part of the execution and especially those who will *not*. Make sure that the proposed team has the knowledge and skills that are needed for the tasks. Wise lean leaders take steps to address any skill gaps early in the process to avoid ugly surprises later.

In particular, this clause must clearly document each participant's level of responsibility and accountability for execution and results. Each person must agree to *accept* the assigned responsibility, and be clear about exactly what is expected of them. Especially in a project context or matrix management environment, be absolutely sure that adding this effort to the existing workload doesn't result in overburdening any one individual. An overloaded individual is a bottleneck waiting to happen.

Not surprisingly, the basic *Who* clause challenges are magnified by the complexities of globalization. As we've already noted, communication among teams scattered around the world is even more challenging than communication among local teams. Effective lean leaders adjust action plan timelines, staffing selections, or other factors to take into account any special multicultural hurdles.

The *What* Clause

To achieve agreement, all parties need to share a common understanding of:

- What is the action that needs to be done?

- What is the goal?

- What does success look like, and how will it be measured?

- What resources are available to use?

In short, *the What clause* defines the current state and the new target state.

Agreements grow stronger as more and more specific details are included. Specific definitions drive absolute clarity and ensure effective execution. Spell out which resources are and are *not* available. Determine if any elements will be outsourced.

The *When* Clause

- When does the overall agreement start? Finish?

- When does each activity start and finish?

Obtaining commitment from all participants about the timeline—especially the final target

date—is crucial. For an agreement to be
effective, everyone involved needs to share clear
expectations about exactly when the new target
state is to be achieved.

Don't forget to include in the timeline (and
the effort estimates) the frequency, duration,
and schedule for team meetings throughout
the life of the agreement. As with any process,
course corrections made early in the execution
of this agreement will prevent larger problems
downstream. Be sure to check for understanding
and compliance at appropriate intervals.

If your agreement involves players in different parts
of the world, don't forget to account for different
time zones in your agreement. I've been caught
more than once by forgetting that other countries
don't have Daylight Savings Time changes!

The *Why* Clause

- Why do things need to change?
- Why now?

- Why is this agreement important to the company? To *me?*

The *What* clause creates a compelling vision of the desired future state. The *Why* clause brings to the surface the underlying situations and issues in the current state that create an imperative for getting to the new target condition. The *Why* clause must help every participant understand the motivation for moving to that future state, both at the organizational level and at the personal level.

Wise lean leaders know that for individuals to make, and especially *sustain,* any significant change from the status quo, they need to understand and embrace "What's in it for me?" and "What do I stand to lose if I don't get on board?" Because you are dealing with people and the communication that happens between them, effectively expressing *why* an action should be taken helps engage and involve those participants in a positive way. The actions that need to happen are no longer an external thing, but have been internalized by each participant.

The *How* Clause

Once you know the current state and can see the new target state you're trying to reach, *the How clause* lays out the action plan:

- How will each step be executed?
- How will the outcome of each step be measured?

The *How* clause drives the team to use any available pre-defined methodologies for executing activity; in the absence of methodologies, the team must come together to hammer out a plan.

Note that both the *What* clause and the *How* clause talk about assessing outcomes. It is vitally important to define and agree on how actions and outcomes will be measured; otherwise, you are opening the door to defects and misunderstandings. Your *What* and *How* efforts are effective only to the degree that you have achieved the new target condition.

The *Where* Clause

- Where will all the action take place?
- Where will we see results?

For many agreements, the *Where* clause may not be needed, because there's only one location involved. However, for larger agreements and global efforts, be sure to specify and document where each action is occurring. Remember, lean thinking tells us to be precise in setting expectations, because that reduces the potential for variance. And not knowing where things are happening could certainly create a problem.

The *What If...* Clause

- What if something doesn't go according to plan (negative or positive)?
- What is the probability of something not going according to plan? What is the pain (or benefit) if that happens?
- How do we minimize or manage the risks?

- What are our contingency plans if
  anything changes?

Anyone with any business experience at all is
familiar with Murphy and his infamous law:
"Anything that *can* go wrong, *will* go wrong!"
The prudent lean leader takes preventative steps
to minimize the damage that Murphy can do
by strengthening agreements with the *What
If...* clause. While anti-Murphy efforts have
always been valuable, globalization has made
them absolutely indispensable. As time, distance,
and complexity keep expanding, the number
and variety of potential points of failure grows
exponentially. The *What If...* clause is no longer a
nice-to-have, it's a necessity.

A required component of every agreement is
the understanding that when *anyone* recognizes
that unexpected changes have the potential to
negatively affect the project and the customer, the
team will regroup, rethink, and establish a new
agreement on a new standard.

In my experience, vast spans of time often elapse between the planning, the actual launch of an activity, and the achievement of the final outcome. For example, when I left an automotive engineering position in 2013, our team was already working on designs for the 2017 car. This added time increases the chances that the laws of entropy and Murphy will thwart our intentions and create unexpected, undesirable results.

The Greek philosopher Heraclitus is famous for saying, "The *only* thing that is constant is change." Therefore, if we believe Heraclitus—and Murphy—then we must conclude that variance to plan is itself a standard. In short, contingencies need to be taken for granted as a crucial part of your agreement. Always.

One proven technique for building contingency plans is to engage participants in a brainstorming session to identify all the many things that might go awry. During this discussion, you may discover that some team members don't yet share a clear understanding of the actions, their responsibilities, the timeline, and so on. This is a great opportunity to sort things out, and gently guide the group toward deeper agreement. Beware of pressuring or using negative influence—that rarely works over the long haul.

Throughout the discussion, summarize and listen for understanding. Make sure everyone contributes. Explain and re-explain anything that isn't understood 100%. Use examples to demonstrate the intent of the action, then listen again, to ensure that the intention of the message sent and the meaning received actually do match. Use this portion of the agreement process to reflect back and forth on each of the steps and clauses to ensure that each player has complete understanding.

To specifically address risk issues, take the brainstormed list of things that might go wrong and engage the group in ranking them. For each item, consider the probability that it might happen, and also the level of pain and disruption that would result if it actually does happen. Items that are low probability and low pain don't require much attention. But for any item that is high probability and high pain, create a countermeasure or contingency plan for how to minimize the probability and/or the pain.

In summary...

As we've seen, *seiketsu* can help organizations achieve the goals of lean communication: all parties involved in the process obtain correctly shared meaning, achieve clear actions, and produce results that are aligned with expectations, goals, and objectives. Make sure your communicators:

- Choose a common language
- Check for variance
- Establish clear agreement

Sustain/*Shitsuke*

I'll bet you know someone who has quit smoking…a dozen times. Or someone who has lost pounds and pounds of excess weight, only to gain them all back and then some. The reality of life is that *sustaining* change takes as much or more energy, focus, and discipline as *attaining* change.

For that matter, even if all you want to do is maintain the status quo, you've still got to exercise discipline to do that; otherwise, entropy will prevail. "If it ain't broke, don't fix it" may be sensible advice in some cases, but if you don't invest in *shitsuke,* things *will* break eventually.

As you apply the magic of lean to transform your communication processes, you and your team members must relentlessly exercise self-discipline and build the habit of consistently using Five S as part of standard work. The idea is to create a cycle that never ends—one where you can *always* find some way to improve your communication process.

In a formal setting, audits can help drive this. One way of conducting a useful audit is to engage an external facilitator or coach who has a solid background in communication and team-building skills. This auditor can observe the team and make known specific factors that are not adding any value in the way that the communication process improvement is actually evolving.

It's human nature for habits and ingrained beliefs to drive us to behave a certain way when we are attempting to communicate with others. Over the years, most of us have grown accustomed to interrupting people before they finish expressing an idea, wandering off in thought while someone is addressing us, using jargon and acronyms that confuse rather than clarify, or any of a hundred other poor communication practices. Once those constraints and negative factors have been pointed out in the previous Five Ss, it takes self-awareness, self-discipline, and deliberate practice to break those habits

Long-term commitment and significant effort are required to achieve the discipline needed to achieve the goal of *shitsuke*—sustaining improved performance. Some individuals may not enjoy the Five S activity or feel that it brings immediate results. Here are two of the hidden benefits of applying Five S to communication processes.

First, the actual activity associated with Five S creates an environment where people from different functional areas may be working together in new ways. Such activity drives improved communication and a sense of teamwork that can build on itself. In particular, mutual respect grows.

Second, the motivation needed to sustain the Five S philosophy requires an understanding that problems and variance *can* be avoided, and that future improvements *can* be achieved. Positive outcomes and reactions from management or customers will provide the reinforcement needed to strengthen the self-discipline even more.

So far in this section, you've seen how the familiar Five Ss of lean manufacturing can be applied to your communication processes. Seiri, seiton, seiso, seiketsu, *and* shitsuke *improve communication in much the same way they improve manufacturing: by reducing waste, sharpening focus, minimizing variances, strengthening relationships, building agreements, standardizing best practices, and continuously improving. Working through the Five S process is excellent preparation for moving into the real heart of continuous process improvement: the Plan-Do-Check-Act cycle.*

The Best-Laid Plans: *Kaizen*/PDCA

Plan-Do-Check-Act is one of the most important philosophies in the lean enterprise. Indeed, if you are a lean practitioner working in business today, your organization probably already sees PDCA as an integral part of the culture, essential to creating an environment of creativity and improvement.

As lean leaders, we can drive improvements in execution by ensuring that communication processes are included in our continuous improvement objectives. The complete enterprise functions as a network of interdependent functional areas, and these must somehow communicate effectively to ensure that there is proper alignment toward common goals.

The PDCA cycle can be very useful in driving improvement throughout the communication process. It serves as a great system to institutionalize continuous learning, limit risks, and perpetuate continuous improvement initiatives. Just as you've done on the manufacturing line, plan a communication improvement, then try it out, keeping a log of good communication outcomes and not-as-expected outcomes (i.e., where variance occurred). Analyze the log data to see if the planned improvement had the desired results, and use the analysis results as the basis for refining the change.

If your communication process improvement efforts involve people who are not already familiar with lean thinking, you may need to teach them our very positive mindset regarding the Check step. Sometimes (frequently!) the Check step reveals that things did not go exactly as planned. Lean thinkers do not the fear the "F word": *failure*.

Those of us immersed in lean thinking understand that to get things right, some mistakes will happen along the way, and that's just part of the process. You may need to coach lean newcomers that there's no such thing as failure—just learning opportunities and teachable moments. Physicist and icon of intelligence Albert Einstein (among others) is credited with defining insanity as "doing the same thing over and over again and expecting different results." Lean practitioners rely on PDCA to avoid that particular brand of insanity.

Rather than worrying about failure, lean communicators learn to focus on collaborative analysis of what happened so that we can learn from it. To do that, we deploy research tools such as fishbone diagrams and the Five Whys, both of which should help expose all forces that have contributed to the outcome, whatever it may be. If some of the forces detected are structural, strategic, or cultural, then these causes belong to management, and must be addressed at that level. That's really the only way to determine how our strategies, policies, and management practices affect the outcome.

People can't read minds; therefore, we can anticipate that something may be lost in the

coding and decoding of a message, and that
the execution of the actions associated with the
intended goals of the message might not have the
result that was originally intended. By learning
from these instances, an organization builds a
knowledge base that can help guide it toward
better results when the next PDCA experiment is
being put together.

This recognition of our human propensity for
communication errors encourages a practice of
designing with tolerances, allowing for natural
forces, and being prepared for potential, inherent
variance. Implementing better communication
practices takes time and takes commitment. But
to *not* commit is a guarantee that someone will eat
your lunch!

As noted earlier, people form companies to serve
customers by providing them with products
and services to fulfill their needs. To do that
successfully, and to ensure that the organization
is evolving in positive ways, the corporate vision
needs to be translated and chunked down to

specific actions. Then these chunks have to be communicated precisely and effectively to each individual, so they fully grasp what needs doing and can go do it. Although vague terms and big words can rally teams around some high-level concepts and ideas, individuals still need specific actions that have a beginning and an end.

As you lead your company's transformation from traditional communication processes to lean communication processes, you may find it helpful to think through the role played by each step of the Plan-Do-Check-Act cycle.

Plan

These planning questions should help you hone your goal and sharpen the aim of your message:

- Who is the message intended for?
  - What background and experience do the receivers have with the topic?
  - How will you address the receivers' culture, skill set, and position?

— Do the receivers have the resources
to understand the message and the
expectation?

— What is the state of mind of the
receivers? Are they overburdened, already
carrying a heavy workload? (*muri, mura*)

— How can you minimize the receivers'
distractions?

• What are you trying to achieve with the
message?

• What information, what data is needed in the
message? What "noise" can be eliminated?

• What action needs to happen with the
message?

• What is the best time to deliver message?

Knowing the answers to these questions allows
you to craft the verbal and non-verbal goals in a
congruent way.

Of course, once you compose a message, you still
must decide which channel will be used to deliver
it. Will you use:

- Email?

- Memo?

- Tweet?

- One-on-one meeting?

- Group meeting?

- Personal phone call?

- Conference call?

- All of the above?

Don't forget the marketing mantra that if you really want people to get your message, you must tell them seven different times in seven different ways.

Finally, and very importantly in the Plan step: how can you induce the participants to express their concerns and doubts *up front*? Having a conversation early in the process about any apprehension helps surface assumptions or underlying preconceptions that anyone may have about the plan. These then become part of the testing that is embedded into PDCA and verified against the outcomes: were the assumptions valid? If yes, confirm their validity; if no, exclude them.

Do

Action is how we get things done. The Do step is the execution portion of communicating the message. Following your plan, you compose the message and deliver it via the chosen channel(s).

Generally speaking, it is preferable to send out small, focused chunks of information in each message. You can safely assume that people need adequate time to process and absorb each message in order to grasp the idea accurately. Sending out a message with too much information or excessive detail tends to confuse the players. Don't let *mura* or *muri* hijack your broadcast. Frankly, many individuals simply tune out lengthy messages or don't read them at all.

Providing messages in small chunks also allows you to introduce one detail at a time, which allows for immediate reaction and discussion of each instance.

When delivering messages in person, be sensitive to the immediate feedback you might get from people via questions, facial expressions, or even the hush in the room. In this sense, you're already easing into the Check step of PDCA as the message elicits a short-term response from the receiver in a very immediate way.

Check

In defining true communication, I made the point that a sender doesn't know whether communication has actually occurred until it is confirmed and verified by the receiver via a feedback loop. The Check step of PDCA actively seeks that feedback. What level of clarity and understanding of the message's meaning did the receiver achieve? Was the receiver able to correctly execute the intended action? In short, how effective was your communication process?

Listeners, take responsibility for your end of the bargain. Reflect back what you heard to confirm that there's no variance!

If the Check step does uncover any variance, then it's time to start digging for root cause:

- Did the message contain the right information? Enough data?

- Was it delivered in the right way at the right time to the right people?

- Were the underlying assumptions or preconceptions correct?

- If not, what went wrong and why?

Remember, finding a variance is not to be treated as a failure, but rather an opportunity to learn and to be more effective in the next cycle...which takes you to the Act step.

Act

Based on what you've learned from the Check step, you can adopt improvements for next time a message must be communicated to stimulate action and achieve goals. Celebrate the positive achievements with the team, and record all new learning to move you toward a new, improved standard.

Always remember: the effectiveness of your message drives effectiveness in the execution.

By adopting PDCA as part of the corporate culture and inserting it in your daily use, you can improve communication and, as a byproduct, execution. Because of ever-increasing diversity and complexity in the workplace, and being aware that communication is a very difficult process to master, it makes good sense to embed this continuous process improvement cycle in your standard processes.

One of the benefits of incorporating PDCA into your communication culture is that it changes an environment where "failure" is punished and, in its place, creates an opening for learning and innovation at every level. More participants will be engaged and become active in problem-solving and adding their creativity to the equation.

By this time, the transformative magic of lean thinking should be making a difference in the quality and effectiveness of the communication process in your organization. Value Stream Mapping, *Five S, and PDCA deliver a powerful punch when removing* muda *from communication. It's time now to add one final ingredient to our Lean Potion #9: the Theory of Constraints.*

Finding the Bottleneck: Theory of Constraints

My personal lean story started with *The Goal*, by Eliyahu Goldratt, where I first learned about the Theory of Constraints. It seems appropriate to come back to that crucial revelation in my message to you by considering what insights that theory can offer in the context of improving communication process effectiveness.

As you lean professionals recall, a system comprises multiple interdependent contributing agents and resources that are linked into a chain, and make up a unified whole that is directed toward specific objectives. At any point in time, at least one part of the system is limiting the overall capacity to achieve more of the intended goal.

That weakest link, once identified, deserves special focus and attention. The system must be managed with this weakest link in mind, because the productivity associated with the specific weak link, is in fact, the productivity of the whole system. This link is labeled as a *system constraint*.

> When an idea out of a person's head reflects a limited point of view, the constraint will be implicit and contained in the messages that are conveyed.

Obviously, that constraint needs to be corrected and improved. But then, once that happens, *another* constraint will emerge, and with it, the need for a process of continuous improvement.

Organizations rely on effective and efficient communication processes for team members to collaborate, to integrate their unique areas, and to be successful in getting things done. Like any system, a communication process will *always* have at least one constraint that can be improved. Correcting these opportunities will lead to an improved overall productivity in a company.

Remember, a communication process is triggered when a thought or idea appears in someone's

head, and that thought or idea needs to be
conveyed if the desired result is going to occur.
By definition, when an idea out of a person's head
reflects a limited point of view, the constraint will
be implicit and contained in the messages that are
conveyed.

Consider these examples of constrained mindsets:

- **Forgetting that the customer pays your
  bills.** Once we forget who we truly work
  for, everything goes downhill. Customer
  expectations and customer satisfaction
  must at all times be kept as the ultimate
  goal of any organization. Not having
  this as the standard for how things
  work in your organization tends to drive
  importance and focus on *internal* players.
  This, in turn, leads to a competitive
  environment within the organization, with
  individuals and functional areas pursuing
  their own interests, which may not align
  with the end customer's needs.

- *Assuming* **that you understood a message clearly**, or that a message you sent was received with 100% of the meaning you intended. This is a foolish point of view that may be an underlying negative factor in many of our daily interactions with others. When an action is undertaken based from a message coming from this point of view, expect variance and *muda*. Lots of it.

- **The belief that you are already "there" and that nothing can be improved.** This mindset may be associated with the need to feel that everything is "in control." In a setting where *not* being in control at all times is a problem, the constraint created builds and builds on itself until something pops. Denying the fact that change is constant and failing to implement systems to support the change are a sure recipe for disaster. Address this constraining mindset through leadership, mentoring, and coaching to make sure everyone at every level understands the imperative of continuous process improvement. Everything can always be improved.

- **Thinking that there is only one *right* way of doing things.** This reflects a scarcity mentality rather than a creative mentality, and is closely related to the previous constraint. You may see this manifested when two or more internal parties, departments, or areas of an organization are communicating based on a win/lose mindset. My way or the highway. Interaction between the parties becomes an arena where departments become rivals looking to get an advantage over one another. Power struggles and one-upmanship become the standard. Ultimately, a tremendous amount of energy is wasted, and the end customer is not in focus. The company loses. The customer loses. Everybody loses.

- **Unclear expectations.** The success of the total organization is directly tied to the effectiveness of the individuals who make up the collective. And for the individuals (and thus the organization) to thrive, they all must know where they fit in, how they contribute, where they add value, and how they drive toward shared goals and objectives. Nobody wins when expectations are hazy and standard processes are not followed. Eventually, the culture becomes infested with deeply engrained preferential treatment of one area over another, leading to entitlement thinking, and arguments about "the way things get done around here."

- **The effect of hierarchy on individual contribution.** When systems in place promote the power of hierarchy over conversation and open dialogue, people may hesitate to participate, and therefore suppress their opinions and concerns.

This may be due to fear of retaliation
or punishment, or just avoidance of
potential embarrassment in front of
their peers or superiors. It may also drive
participants to "retire in place," using the
situation as an excuse to not contribute
any additional effort.

In systems where this is tolerated and
no alternatives are present to encourage
people to participate, the organization
constrains the potential it has from every
employee at every level—the eighth form
of *muda*.

- **Playing the blame game instead of
  using systemic root cause analysis.** This
  constraint is present in cultures where the
  immediate response to a problem is to find
  a scapegoat—*any* scapegoat. Lean thinking
  teaches us to "blame the *process*, not the
  person," and to bring the cold, hard logic
  of analytical thinking to bear when there's
  a situation to address. In contrast, the

blaming mindset perpetuates a culture of unaccountability: I'll get blamed regardless of the facts, so why should I care? The fear of finger-pointing also fosters a "play it safe" attitude throughout the organization, squelching experimentation and innovation.

- **Talent that does not fit the organization's culture.** Because change is constant, even good organizations have a flux of people coming and going. That means new people are periodically coming in, trying to understand and, presumably, fit in with the unwritten rules of behavior, the communication styles, the attitudes, and all the other intangibles that make up the culture of the organization. An individual who can't or won't make the effort to fit becomes grit in the gears, creating constraints in many directions.

The Human Resources function needs to be aware of the impact that mismatched talent can have on the overall efficiency of the company, and how it is, in fact, a constraint. As a preventive measure, HR can implement a *poka-yoke* in the hiring process by using psychometric assessment tools in addition to having a robust interview and selection process.

As you deal with constraints like these in your organization's communication flows, consider using a little Lean Potion #9 to clean out the clogs.

Congratulations, O Intrepid Reader! Having made it this far, you have now mixed your own fresh batch of Lean Potion #9, compounding the familiar tools from

Lean Lingo

A poka-yoke device is one that prevents incorrect parts from being made or assembled, or easily identifies a flaw or error.

the shop floor with a slightly altered perspective on what communication is and how it takes place. Are you ready to take on the next leg of the journey?

Chapter 4
The *Tip* of the Tip of
the Iceberg

The toughest problems to solve are those that
lurk and hide, unseen. Invisible to the naked
eye. Because we do not see the waves of today's
cellular phone systems, the exchange of bits as we
upload files to "the cloud," or transmit a simple
message from one person to another, it's easy to
assume that things are working correctly, even
though they may not be.

Lean thinking applied to communication
processes can and does bring issues to the surface
so that they can be viewed and analyzed for
continuous improvement and correctives. This is
part of the magic potion of transformation—from
the unseen to the "staring right at you."

The ideas set out in this book are intended as introductions to what is truly just the *tip* of the tip of the iceberg.

What ties everything together is *communication.*

Differences in our cultures, backgrounds, or language can be harnessed toward a synergistic approach, instead of one that creates barriers that lead to *muda.* Respect for people is one of the pillars of lean. By having the right conversations and working together to solve all problems, universal respect can become a reality.

Every workplace today needs people who've mastered three basic skill sets: communication, teamwork, and problem-solving. In my opinion, these precious skill sets are not developed in our universities in a congruent way that is beneficial in the situations facing today's complex business environments

Communication is a process, and process-based solutions *do* exist. Many consulting companies can provide the analysis and training to overcome some of the gaps left by the lack of attention to this need. Unfortunately, the day-to-day, chase-your-tail rat race too often prevents us from acknowledging the need and seeking out solutions to our communication challenges.

If you suspect that your company is harboring such situations, I challenge you to start a conversation about it by establishing a good metric for the impact and costs that communication-related *muda* might be generating.

Next, establish a good process to fix the issue. Consider, for example, the familiar andon cord. In his book *The Toyota Way*, author Jeffrey K. Liker talks about *jidoka*—the concept of stopping the process to build in quality.

To explain *jidoka* and how it relates to employee empowerment, Liker includes this insightful quote from Alex Warren, former Executive Vice President, Toyota Motor Corporation, Kentucky:

... we give [employees] the power to push buttons or pull cords—called "andon cords"—which can bring our entire **assembly line** to a halt. Every team member has the responsibility to stop the **line** every time they see something that is out of standard. That's how we put the responsibility for quality in the hands of our team members. They feel the responsibility—they feel the power. They know they count.[16]

Now, read the quote again. This time, think about the flow of communication processes, and substitute in the word *conversation* when you read *assembly line* or *line*. See if you don't learn something about how this lean concept could prevent miscommunication and misunderstanding.

Imagine the *muda* that would magically vanish if everyone in your organization, regardless of level or title, confidently pulled the metaphorical andon cord, stopping the flow of conversation long

---

[16] from *The Toyota Way*, by Jeffrey K. Liker. New York, NY: McGraw-Hill, 2004.

enough to make sure that there are no defects in the understanding, and that the agreements are up to standard.

In some cultures, speaking up is not well received. In settings where these social norms exist, the andon cord concept is a great device to create a "stop and evaluate" moment when a message is not clear, and to ensure no misunderstandings are present. In some cases, it may help to have a skilled facilitator assist with meetings. Facilitators will pull the andon cord for you, and make it a point to show you those opportunities where communication can be improved.

In a similar way, imagine how much wasted time and energy could be reclaimed by eliminating unnecessary discussions where individuals are trying to score points, show off what they know, or "win" an argument. Actually, everybody loses at the end of the day when this kind of nonsense blocks the open exchange of ideas and diminishes the team's progress toward reaching mutual understanding needed to meet the customer's needs.

In the meantime, and while the corporate world catches up with the challenges of communication, consider that as a lean practitioner, you have the language advantage, the philosophy of continuous improvement, and the tools to solve many of these problems.

> As a lean practitioner, you have the language advantage, the philosophy of continuous improvement, and the tools to solve many of these communication problems.

For the diligent reader, the ideas in Lean Potion #9 are intended to serve as a springboard for you and your company—one that moves you toward creating a systemic set of solutions to identify problems and costly *muda* stemming from snags that exist in your communication processes.

CHAPTER 5
YOUR MISSION, SHOULD YOU
DECIDE TO ACCEPT IT

Our vision is to drive the use of lean philosophies
deep into every aspect of managing and leading
our companies. But massive culture shifts like
this don't just happen by magic—they take
strong, sustained leadership at every level of the
organization.

We thought it might be helpful for you to
understand our modest goal for this first
round in what we hope will be a continuing
conversation: simply to provide you with a
thought-provoking vision for transforming
yet another aspect of the global supply
chain—communication—through the power of
lean thinking.

This first book focuses on stories and analogies to illustrate our ideas. We confess right up front that many potent concepts, like A3 problem-solving, and classic constructs, like detailed case studies, are *not* included in this work. After all, how much stuff can you stuff into one book, and still deliver a quick and engaging read? KISS—Keep it Short and Simple—right?

Also, we humbly acknowledge that

Lean Lingo

"...we have observed a number of lean transformations in companies of different sizes in which the point of origin was mid-level managers and where quiet leadership was effective without the need for shouting or theatrics. But still, a **leader**—someone who will take personal responsibility for change—is essential. No organization has ever undergone dramatic and comprehensive change without someone somewhere, softly or in a loud voice, taking the lead."
~*Womack and Jones, in* Lean Thinking

in some chapters we're being very casual with the term *tools*, and we do appreciate that it is only the sum of the methodologies, including some tools, that make up a complete lean management system. Optimists that we are, we expect to engage with you to continue this conversation! We'd love to include ***your*** case studies, practical applications, and success stories in a follow-up volume.

Mid-level lean practitioners can lead the charge by taking lean off the shop floor and educating key players in the C-suite about how to reengineer communication processes using this well-documented and successful system. It's a natural pathway toward reducing costs gaining a competitive edge and creating more jobs.

So don't just sit there! People make things happen, and to keep them coordinated, you need effective communication processes. Logically, if you successfully apply your lean understanding to those processes, then the coordinated efforts of people in your enterprise should improve.

Lean management and lean communication are
the next wave of lean transformation— *if you are
bold enough to* **take the lead! Take responsibility!**

*Did you get my meaning? Or is there a variance?
We invite you to see additional content and join the
conversation at LeanPotion9.com You have nothing
to lose… except* muda*!*

BIBLIOGRAPHY

- Clark, Nicola. "The Airbus saga: Crossed wires and a multibillion-euro delay – Business – International Herald Tribune." December 11, 2006. www.nytimes.com. The New York Times. http://www.nytimes.com/2006/12/11/business/worldbusiness/11 iht-airbus.3860198.html?_r=0.

- Covey, Stephen R. *The 7 Habits of Highly Effective People®*. New York, NY: Simon & Schuster. 1989.

- Goatham, Robert and Brig Henry. "Airbus – A380 – Why Projects Fail." Calleam. com. April 20, 2013. Calleam Consulting Ltd. http://calleam.com/WTPF/?p=4700.

- Goldratt, Eliyahu. *The Goal*. Great Barrington, MA: The North River Press, 1984.

- Liker, Jeffrey K. *The Toyota Way*. New York, NY: McGraw-Hill, 2004.
- Newton, Randall S. "Lessons for All CAD Users from the Airbus CATIA Debacle." AECNews.com. September 29, 2006. http://aecnews.com/articles/2035.aspx.
- Rother, Mike, and John Shook. *Leaning to See: Value Stream Mapping to Add Value and Eliminate* Muda. Cambridge, MA: The Lean Enterprise Institute, Inc., 2003.
- Rothman, Andrea. "Airbus Vows Computers Will Speak Same Language After A380 Delay." www.Bloomberg.com. September 28, 2006. Bloomberg L.P. http://www.bloomberg.com/apps/news?pid=newsarchive&sid=aSGkIYVa9IZk.
- Stewart, Thomas A. *Intellectual Capital: the New Wealth of Nations.* New York, NY: Doubleday, 1999.
- Womack, James P., and Daniel T. Jones. *Lean Solutions.* New York, NY: Free Press, 2005.
- ———. *Lean Thinking.* New York, NY: Free Press, 2003.

Made in the USA
Charleston, SC
07 March 2017